BETTER BIDDING
IN 15 MINUTES—
EXPERT BIDDING
IN A WEEK

by Howard Schenken

INTRODUCTION BY *Albert H. Morehead,*
Bridge Editor, *The New York Times*

SIMON AND SCHUSTER, NEW YORK, 1963

To my wife, Bee

Contents

PART IV: THE SYSTEMS COMPARED

PART V: APPENDIX

Introduction

I first met Howard Schenken at four o'clock in the morning. He would not remember it; I do. It was in a restaurant called the C & L. The C & L might have captured the bridge players' business on its own, because it was convenient to New York's bridge clubs and it was open all night; but that was not the reason the bridge players went there. The bridge players went there because Schenken might be there.

Until that occasion at 4 A.M. I had never heard of Howard Schenken. I was not yet a New Yorker; I was a Southern boy enamored of bridge and on infrequent visits to New York I would play bridge and talk bridge all night rather than sleep. The other players, when my game broke up, took me along to eat with them and that is how I met Schenken.

It was not really a meeting; or, if it was, it was an odd sort of meeting. Maybe we were introduced, probably we weren't; anyway, we did not exchange two words. But I was impressed. What impressed me, since I already knew what bridge players are like, was that all the other bridge players asked Schenken for his opinions and when he gave his opinions they never argued.

Not too long afterward I became a New Yorker and ever since I have known what the minor experts at the C & L knew then.

I am firmly and irrevocably convinced that Howard Schenken is the greatest bridge player that ever lived. This conviction makes me part of a big majority group. When a national magazine polled the nation's experts some years ago to discover the best bridge player, Schenken won hands down. The *Bridge World* magazine unabashedly blurbed a Schenken article, "An Interview with America's Greatest Player." My friend and partner Waldemar von Zedtwitz, when a brash newcomer at the Cavendish Club had questioned a Schenken dictum, exclaimed with righteous indignation, "Can you imagine that ignoramus setting himself up against the best bridge player in the world!" And at that time von Zedtwitz himself had an acknowledged place in the top five.

The youngsters who so easily master, through tutelage and example, the polished technique of championship bridge in the 1960s have no idea that much of what they take for granted today was unknown until Schenken showed how. Maybe they would have worked it out for themselves, maybe they wouldn't, but the fact remains.

Despite my early acquaintance with Schenken, I was amazed when years later I accidentally discovered that Schenken can also write.

At the time that I discovered this, I am sure Schenken didn't know it himself. War had scattered and death had decimated Schenken's famous Four Aces team, and I was asked as a favor to edit the syndicated bridge column that the Four Aces had contracted to write. The articles came in to me written by Schenken in a big round schoolboy hand on a big ruled schoolboy's tablet. I looked and looked and looked for something that needed changing, but for the life of me I couldn't find anything but a comma here and semicolon there.

I was surprised again many years later when Schenken asked me to look over the manuscript of this book. This time I was surprised because I had thought Schenken would never get around to writing a bridge book. It didn't surprise me at all that the manuscript was very well written—exactly the style and exactly the approach that the average bridge player would ask for.

What about the bridge system that Howard Schenken is presenting in his remarkably lucid style?

Considering what I have already written in this Introduction, it would be easy for me to say that anything the world's best bridge player says is good enough for me; but I am not quite so naive. As an experienced player, I first had to consider everything Schenken wrote and form my own conclusions. If I had been in violent disagreement I would have said so and the publishers of this book would not have asked me to write this Introduction.

I got the enviable job of writing this Introduction because I can honestly say that I like what Schenken has to say.

The Schenken System starts with the strong one club bid, the brilliant and profound idea of the inventor of contract bridge, Harold Vanderbilt, who propounded it in early times when contract bridge was not even proved to be viable. The club convention was not immediately successful, because the average player abhors artificial bids, but the principle behind the club convention has been winning world championships for years.

Every bidding system is built upon a basic principle. Once the system is built, its parts are so closely interlocked that no part can be changed without some effect on every other part.

On the foundation of the club bid for strong hands, and limited bids for other hands, Howard Schenken has built the kind of system one should expect from the greatest player.

Let me quote a sentence from an article I wrote long ago, in 1945: "If an angry bridge-table argument ends with the injunction 'Go get yourself a partner,' nine out of ten experts will go get Schenken."

Well, here is your opportunity to play the system Schenken's partner plays.

ALBERT MOREHEAD

New York
1963

PART I

♠

THE BASIC SYSTEM

1: *Why We Need a New System*

In my opinion, American bidding is obsolete and outmoded, inaccurate and ineffective.

I did not arrive at this conclusion hastily. In fact, it took me quite a few years while the evidence was piling up, although the flaws were always there for everyone to see.

Let's review a little bridge history.

Contract bridge was invented by an American, Harold S. Vanderbilt, in 1925; and Americans were the first to play it. This gave us a head start, and for many years we were superior to any other nation.

I can make that statement from personal knowledge. As captain of the Four Aces team, which won nearly every major event during the 1930s, I participated in the first true world championship in 1935, and we easily defeated a French team which had won the European championship. Then, when world-championship play was resumed in 1950 (after a long time-out for World War II) and the United States won three times in a row—against English, Swedish, and Italian teams—I was a member of all three victorious American teams. I was convinced then that the Europeans were no match for us.

How times have changed! The year 1955 started a sequence of eight consecutive years in which the United States lost the world championship, twice to France, once to Britain, and five times to Italy, which has dominated the field since 1957.

Why this lamentable record?

Is it in card playing? No, for expert card play has not changed to any great extent. Surely we have as many top-notch card players as the nations that have beaten us so regularly. In fact, the Europeans who have beaten us freely acknowledge that we have *more* good card players.

The plain unvarnished truth is that they have consistently outbid us! While they have been busy developing and perfecting accurate bidding methods, we have smugly stood pat.

The best European players condescendingly express great admiration for American experts "who do so well with their antiquated bidding methods." What's wrong with American bridge at the international level is wrong at every level, because the same antiquated methods are used.

"Standard American" and How It Works—or Doesn't

The most popular system in this country is called, for want of a better name, Standard American. Its distinguishing feature is a super-strong game-forcing two bid, usually at least 25 high-card points, although it can be slightly less with a six- or seven-card suit. Hence suit bids of one can be, and often are, very strong hands, often 20 or more high-card points. There are several other systems in vogue, but they are mere extensions of Standard American. They add a few gadgets, or they change a few requirements, but they all have one thing in common with Standard American: the opening bid of one in a suit is almost unlimited.

Inasmuch as the opening bid in the great majority of deals is one in a suit, if that bid doesn't work you might as well throw the rest of the system away.

In Standard American, an opening bid of one diamond might be made on:

♠ A xx   ♡ xx   ◇ A J 10 xx   ♣ K xx

which has 12 points in high cards and a good five-card suit. But according to the authorities on Standard American bidding, one diamond should also be bid on:

♠ xx   ♡ A K Q   ◇ A K xxx   ♣ A K J

which has 24 points, twice the point count of the first hand!

This vast difference in strength has a serious effect on all responses and rebids.

1. The partner of the opening bidder must strain to keep the bidding open with very little, in the hope that the opener has one of these gigantic hands.

2. After the response of, say, one spade to one diamond, opener is completely at sea as to whether responder has very little, a fair hand, a good hand, or a very good hand.

3. On those sad occasions when opener's partner cannot find any response, everyone within earshot knows he has nothing and therefore may bid freely.

There are further disadvantages. Consider these hands, bid by two American experts:

OPENER	RESPONDER
♠ A K x	♠ J xxxx
♡ K Q 10 9 x	♡ J x
◇ A K Q x	◇ J xx
♣ x	♣ Q J x

This was the actual bidding:

OPENER	RESPONDER
1 ♡	1 ♠
3 ◇	3 NT
Pass	

A club was the natural opening lead, and declarer's stopper was quickly removed. Though spades were divided 3–2, the queen failed to drop. Thus the contract was set two tricks, although four spades or four hearts would easily have been made.

Each player blamed the other for the disaster.

Opener said that after his jump rebid of three diamonds, responder should have rebid his five-card suit, as opener had implied strength in spades. Opener contended that responder's second bid of three notrump denied a five-card suit and showed two stoppers in clubs, the unbid suit.

This was responder's rebuttal: Opener's jump rebid showed a very strong hand, but might not include strong spade support. Therefore, responder maintained, he could not rebid a weak five-card spade suit; he had to show his sure club stopper by bidding three notrump. However, responder said, with a singleton club and A-K-x of spades opener should have bid four spades over three notrump.

This argument will probably go on indefinitely. Both players can produce hands to prove they were right. And I agree with them!

Responder might have bid one spade on something like:

♠ J xxx   ♡ J x   ◇ J xx   ♣ K J 10 x

where three notrump would be the proper contract. Or opener might have held:

♠ A x   ♡ K Q 10 9 x   ◇ A K Q x   ♣ K x

where at least nine tricks at notrump were sure, but four spades would have no chance.

I assure you these are two fine players, winners of many national championships. So whose fault was it?

There is only one culprit—the opening bid itself! What then is the answer? It stands out like a sore thumb! Simply to limit the strength of the opening bid of one of a suit.

In Italy, France, and England, most experts today sharply limit the opening suit bid.

An example will illustrate the various methods:

♠ A K J xx   ♡ x   ◇ A Q 10 x   ♣ A Q x   20 pts.

In all popular American systems this tremendous hand is a mere one spade opening bid. Italian, French, and British players among others have seen the folly of this and have improvised bids which limit the strength of an opening suit bid.

In Italy all strong hands are opened with one club, which is unlimited in strength. This of course is an artificial bid. It was originated many years ago by Harold Vanderbilt. The Italian System is directly descended from the Vanderbilt Club.

The Italian System is good, but difficult to play even with a fine partner. Two average players would only flounder, because the system contains a whole series of artificial bids, responses, and rebids which must be memorized.

Furthermore, the Italian opening bid of one notrump is artificial, describing a minimum opening bid, usually with five clubs. Thus they have no natural opening one notrump bid, and lose all the valuable information this bid imparts. Other countries use semi-forcing and one-round-forcing suit two bids which have some virtues and some defects.

The New Simplified Club Bid

Weighing the pros and cons of all the systems, I decided several years ago that a simplified forcing one club bid to show a strong hand, with limited opening bids in the other suits, was the cure for the lack of accuracy in American bidding. I discovered quickly that placing each type of hand in a narrowly limited category not only made bidding more accurate—it also made it much easier.

In developing the system I had two enthusiastic assistants—my wife, Bee, and Peter Leventritt, my partner in major team-of-four matches. A number of other experts have tested the system with success.

Leventritt and I started playing it in the summer of 1960, when we won the National Masters' Team-of-Four Championship. This victory entitled us to play on the United States team for the world championship. In Buenos Aires in April, 1961, our team defeated the French and Argentine teams, but lost to the Italians. In 1961 and 1962, Leventritt and I again reached the finals of the Masters' Team-of-Four.

While preparing the manuscript of this book, I enlisted the advice of Lawrence Rosler, who is a high-ranking member of the new, younger generation of American experts.

I believe that average, as well as advanced, players can improve their bidding immensely by using the new Schenken System. Young players, who seem nowadays to expend their talents on new gadgets to patch up the current unsuccessful systems, may decide instead to devote their efforts to a bidding method both simple and logical. And our experts, if they are gracious enough to give the Schenken System a thorough try, may at long last bring the world championship back to America.

Let me tell you of a satisfying experience I had with one of our expert players. First I must take you back to 1934. I had twice won the National Masters' Pairs Championship for the von Zedtwitz Gold Cup. Both times my partner was David Bruce, a member of the Four Aces.

Because a player who won the trophy three times would gain permanent possession, Bruce and I agreed to split up. He played with Oswald Jacoby, I with Richard L. Frey, both members of the Four Aces.

Frey and I won the tournament, and I received the trophy. Although since then we have collaborated for many years on a nationally syndicated bridge column, that was the last time we played as partners.

In November, 1962, we were both in Bermuda for a regional tournament. I agreed to play with him in the pair championships—provided he played my system. As he had never played it before, I coached him for about fifteen minutes. Then we went out and won the tournament.

Right now I am thinking of all the victories we might have won in the twenty-eight years we did not play together. But then again, we would not have had the System to make it possible.

You Can Play the Schenken System with Any Partner

I know, of course, that you—the reader—may not have the

least personal interest in who wins international championships. Like everyone else, you want to win in the game *you* play in, whether rubber bridge or the local duplicate.

I am confident that from the chapters that follow you can learn how to win, how to avoid the pitfalls of Standard American bidding, and how to bid better than you ever have before.

But maybe you will say, "Your system sounds good to me; but what use is it if my partner doesn't know it too?"

My answer is this:

If possible, get your partner to learn the system too, so you can develop a complete partnership. Fifteen minutes should be ample time to teach him the fundamentals.

If he can't be bothered to spend the fifteen minutes, *you* can still play the most important parts of the system with him. It won't take much more than a minute to tell him this:

"1. My opening one club bid is artificial and shows a strong hand, 17 points or more, 14 points with a powerful one- or two-suit hand.

"2. If you have less than 9 points, respond one diamond.

"3. After your negative response of one diamond, if I rebid without jumping you may pass; if I jump in a suit you must respond again.

"4. If you have 9 points or more, you make your natural response (with a diamond suit you must respond two diamonds). After your 'positive' response, we may not pass short of game, since our combined hands must contain at least 26 points.

"5. My opening one bids in the other suits are limited to at most 16 points. Don't bother to keep the bidding open on trash— you need 8 points or more.

"6. If I open two clubs, it shows an ordinary one club bid with at least a good, five-card club suit.

"7. My opening three club bid shows a solid suit with 6 to 7 playing tricks.

"8. My notrumps, takeout doubles, preempts, etc., are the same as yours."

This summary, brief as it is, should suffice to launch you on your new bidding career with a reasonably intelligent partner. *You can play the Schenken System even if he doesn't.* I have proved this many times in rubber bridge games, with most profitable results.

Of course, for the best results it is desirable for your partner also to play the Schenken System. But I am confident that this will soon happen.

Your partner will see how well you are doing, and how easy it is to bid accurately with you. Soon thereafter he will be playing the full system with you.

Hand Evaluation in the Schenken System

High-card points: ace = 4, king = 3, queen = 2, jack = 1.

As opening bidder, for a suit contract, add 1 point for the fourth card of any suit (Q-x-x-x, J-10-x-x, or better). Add an additional point for the fifth card of any suit, and 2 points for every card over five.

The point count undervalues a long solid suit or two very strong suits. Therefore, *count your playing tricks.*

As opening bidder or responder at notrump, use the high-card point evaluation, which is reasonably accurate.

When raising partner's suit, holding one or more trump honors, add 1 point. For each doubleton, add 1 point. For a singleton, add 3 points (2 points holding only three trumps). For a void, add 5 points (4 points holding only three trumps).

2: *One Club Forcing*

The crux of the Schenken System is the use of a forcing opening bid of one club to show a strong hand. The bid is artificial in that the hand may or may not have long clubs.

There are two types of strong hands on which the one club opening should be made:

1. *Balanced strong hands:* 17 to 22 high-card points.

    ♠ xx   ♡ A J 10 x   ◇ A Q xx   ♣ A Q x   17 pts.

This hand has the required number of points for a one notrump opening, but the worthless doubleton in spades makes that bid inadvisable. Many players open one notrump whenever they have the right point count, regardless of some blatant weakness such as a worthless doubleton. Using their bidding methods they cannot describe the hand otherwise. Often they end up lucky, but this type of notrump frankly makes me shudder.

    ♠ A J x   ♡ A Q x   ◇ K J xx   ♣ A xx   19 pts.

Hands of 19 or 20 points fall in the "twilight zone." They are too strong for one notrump, but too weak for two notrump. In Standard American such a hand is usually opened one club. This is unrealistic, particularly at match points. One club passed out figures to be bad, for partner may be short in clubs, and the hand is best suited to notrump. The opponents have the option to bid if they wish, or to pass if they like clubs. If partner responds, opener must now bid *two* notrump, and may well be too high.

This problem does not exist in the Schenken System. Responder may not pass one club—with a weak hand he bids one diamond. Opener then bids *one* notrump, showing 19 or 20 points, and responder is free to pass. It might prove hard to win even seven tricks.

♠ K xxxx   ♥ A K J   ♦ A K Q   ♣ xx   20 pts.

If you open one spade (playing Standard American) and partner passes, you may go down, yet be able to make part-score or even game in another suit. Even if partner finds a response of one notrump, you might land in the wrong contract. You would have to bid three notrump, but might belong in hearts or diamonds.

If you open one club (playing the Schenken System) the problem dissolves. You can now rebid one spade, and partner can show a suit with ease.

♠ A K Q x   ♥ K Q xxx   ♦ A J   ♣ xx   19 pts.

Playing Standard American, you open one heart, planning to reverse into spades. Suppose partner holds:

♠ J xxxx   ♥ xx   ♦ Q xx   ♣ xxx

Will he bid on only three points? I doubt it.

If you open the Schenken one club, over partner's one diamond response, you bid one heart, and he has no problem about bidding one spade.

♠ A Q xx   ♥ A K xx   ♦ K Q x   ♣ A x   22 pts.

With 21 or 22 points opener bids one club, then jumps to two notrump. With an even stronger hand he opens two diamonds (to be discussed in Chapter 14).

2. *Unbalanced strong hands.* By this time it should be clear that one club shows a hand on which you expect to make game

with a modicum of support. Certain strong one-suiters and two-suiters fall into this category. Sometimes these fine hands have fewer than 17 high-card points, but they should never have fewer than 14 points.

♠ A K Q J xx   ♡ x   ◇ K J x   ♣ A xx   18 pts.

♠ K Q J xxx   ♡ x   ◇ A x   ♣ A K xx   17 pts.

Bid one club. Very little is needed for game. In fact, some experts open one club on such hands, with no partnership understanding, because they are afraid partner might pass a one spade opening. I also bid one club—forcing—and partner *knows* I have a strong hand.

♠ x   ♡ A K Q xxx   ◇ A Q 10 x   ♣ xx   15 pts.

Bid one club. The diamond king may be enough for game.

♠ A K 10 9 x   ♡ A Q J xx   ◇ xx   ♣ x   14 pts.

A minimum one club bid in high cards, on a major two-suiter. Game may be made with three hearts to the king and a doubleton spade or, with luck, as little as three spades to the queen and a doubleton heart.

♠ xx   ♡ x   ◇ A K 10 9 x   ♣ A Q J xx   14 pts.

Bid one diamond. Here partner will need enough strength to respond freely in order for you to make game.

Comparison with the "Short Club"

Oddly enough, while disdaining to play "one club forcing," some players may open a "short club" on a very strong hand. I have seen renowned experts bid one club on such hands as those quoted earlier:

♠ A K Q J xx   ♡ x   ◇ K J x   ♣ A xx   18 pts.

♠ K Q J xxx   ♡ x   ◇ A x   ♣ A K xx   17 pts.

I am morally certain these experts have no private understanding whereby their partners *must* make some response. Partner does not know that they have a very strong hand, for they might also bid one club on a minimum hand such as:

♠ xx   ♡ A J x   ◇ xxx   ♣ A Q J xx   12 pts.

These experts believe these strong hands are not worth a game-force opening. They know it is easier (and safer) to respond to one club than to any other bid, and they fear that partner may pass a "normal" one spade opening, yet they may still have enough for game. With many players, passing partner's one *club* opening just isn't done.

If it pays to bid one club on such strong hands—despite the risk of partner's passing and despite the completely distorted picture responder will get if the auction continues—isn't it obviously to the advantage of the partnership to agree in advance that one club shows a strong hand and may not be passed?

The value of the information that the partnership exchanges when the bidding is opened with one club cannot be overestimated. Suppose the words "I have a good hand" were substituted for one club. In turn, suppose partner could reply "I have a poor hand" instead of bidding one diamond. You now "open" the bidding with one spade.

You already know that your partner does not have a good hand but he knows that you do. It is bound to be easier to reach your best contract than if you had started out with one spade, which in standard practice might be anywhere from 12 to 24 points.

To those readers who prefer "natural bidding," I readily admit that the forcing opening bid of one club and the negative response of one diamond are wholly artificial. I like to ask advocates of "natural bidding," do you play Blackwood or Stayman? Blackwood is an *artificial* convention asking for aces, and is played almost universally. Stayman is an *artificial* club bid after an opening notrump, for finding a major-suit fit, and is played by millions, including almost all experts. I sincerely believe that the one-club-forcing method simplifies bidding as far as is possible in this difficult game, while enhancing its accuracy.

Additional Advantages of One Club Forcing

First I will indicate the advantages when one club is opened. Partner knows immediately that you have a strong hand. You can proceed unhurriedly to the best contract, whether it be a part-score, game, or slam. And if the opponents get frisky, partner or you can make a satisfying penalty double.

Now for the very valuable negative information that partner derives when one club is *not* opened. If you open one diamond, one heart, or one spade, your hand is definitely limited. For one thing you have fewer than 17 points in high cards, for with 17 or more you would open one club. Nor can you have a powerful one-suit or two-suit hand with 14 to 16 points, for again you would open one club. So partner does not have to strain to keep the bidding open, and can pass holding up to 8 points (lacking distributional advantages) without fear of missing game.

This brings up four more advantages:

1. You can open with one of a suit somewhat lighter than in other systems, except when your one bid is in clubs.

2. This gives you the advantage of attack and puts the opponents in a defensive position.

3. It often informs partner of the best opening lead.

4. If your partner passes a suit bid other than one club, he may still have defensive values. The opponents therefore cannot reopen with the impunity they enjoy against other systems, for your partner may be able to make a penalty double. And if an opponent becomes declarer, he cannot locate all the high cards.

3: *Getting to the Best Contract After One Club*

If you open one club and the next player passes, partner must make the negative one diamond response unless he has at least 9 points in high cards, including at least 1½ honor tricks (an ace and a king; a king-queen and a king; three kings; or an ace-queen, preferably heading a long suit). Two aces are enough for a positive response even with only 8 points.*

I take as the first example a hand from one of Charles Goren's newspaper quizzes. Partner opens one spade (playing Standard American) and you hold:

♠ 10   ♡ Q 10 7 2   ◊ K J 8 6 4 2   ♣ 7 5   6 pts.

The only acceptable response according to Goren is one notrump. This is in effect an artificial response, because your hand is quite unsuitable for notrump. Obviously you would prefer to bid diamonds, but this bid is barred, as you lack the 10 points in high cards needed to respond at the two-level.

After your one notrump response, partner makes a jump rebid of three spades. The question is, "What do you do now?" Goren's answer is, "Pass."

I agree. Any other action is fraught with danger. You dare not show your diamond suit at the high level of four. If partner does

---

* The positive responses considered here are one heart and one spade, two clubs, and two diamonds. Special responses and rebids to show solid or semisolid suits will be discussed in Chapter 12, which deals with slam bidding.

not fit diamonds, the opponents may double this and any subsequent bid.

Goren does not show the opening bidder's hand, which might have been any of these:

(1) ♠ K Q 9 xxx ♡ K xx ◇ x ♣ A K J   16 pts.

(2) ♠ A K xxxx ♡ A J xx ◇ A x ♣ x   16 pts.

(3) ♠ A Q 9 xxx ♡ x ◇ A xx ♣ A K x   17 pts.

The first hand will probably make three spades. The second hand should play at four hearts. On the third hand five diamonds is a virtual certainty, and six is a reasonable contract.

I would like to emphasize this observation: If a player holds a hand on which, playing Standard American, he could make a jump rebid after a one notrump response, he has an opening bid of one club in the Schenken System. Let's see how the bidding would go if the opening bid were one club.

(1)	OPENER	RESPONDER
	1 ♣	1 ◇
	1 ♠	2 ◇
	2 ♠	Pass

Opener's one spade rebid is not forcing. If responder has a bust and no long suit, he should pass. If opener wants to be *sure* that partner keeps the bidding open he must jump in a suit. None of the hands shown above is strong enough to force a second response. Note that the final contract is lower and safer, because having opened one club, opener need not jump to show a strong hand.

(2)	OPENER	RESPONDER
	1 ♣	1 ◇
	1 ♠	2 ◇
	2 ♡	4 ♡
	Pass	

Opener can afford to show his hearts rather than rebid spades. Having shown a strong hand, he need not fear missing game if partner passes.

(3)

OPENER	RESPONDER
1 ♣	1 ◇
1 ♠	2 ◇
4 ◇	5 ◇
Pass	

I agree with Goren that it is too risky to mention the broken diamond suit for the first time at the four level. But when the opening bid is one club, responder—having disclosed his weakness by his one diamond response—has the opportunity to show his diamonds at the level of two. This is neither a high nor a dangerous level, and a fit can be found for game.

Let me stress again the advantages gained on these three hands as a direct result of the one club opening bid:

1. Opener need not jump-rebid on a strong one-suiter, taking the risk of getting overboard on a misfit.
2. Opener can show a second suit at a low level.
3. Responder can show *his* suit at a low level.

Let's now consider a hand already discussed in Chapter 1 (p. 17).

OPENER	RESPONDER
♠ A K x	♠ J xxxx
♡ K Q 10 9 x	♡ J x
◇ A K Q x	◇ J xx
♣ x	♣ Q J x

This was the bidding by two experts:

OPENER	RESPONDER
1 ♡	1 ♠
3 ◇	3 NT
Pass	

Result—down two tricks.
Our bidding with these hands would be:

OPENER	RESPONDER
1 ♣	1 ◊
2 ♡	2 ♠
4 ♠	Pass

Result—four spades bid and made.

With 21 points in high cards including two good suits opener is strong enough to *force* partner to respond again, hence the *jump* rebid of two hearts. Responder's bid of two spades necessarily shows a five-card suit. If, for example, he had only four spades and another club or diamond, his response over two hearts would be two notrump. With another heart he would bid three hearts.

If responder held a hand like

♠ Q xxxx   ♡ xx   ◊ xxx   ♣ A xx

he would bid on toward slam, for opener has contracted for game opposite what might be a bust.

Now let's take another hand. East-West had 40 on score.

WEST	EAST
♠ A xx	♠ xx
♡ A K xxx	♡ Q xxx
◊ A x	◊ xx
♣ A xx	♣ K Q xxx

This was the bidding:

WEST	EAST
1 ♡	2 ♡
3 ♡	Pass

Result—made game but missed a slam. True, West bid beyond game, but what could East do? If four hearts were needed for game he might have ventured that, but holding no aces could he encourage a slam? He passed, even as you or I might.

Various suggestions, including a series of cue bids by West, were put forth as to how the pair might have reached their almost cold slam, but this was "after the fact." In actuality the bidding system was not equipped to cope with the problem. Here is how the hand might be bid after a one club opening:

WEST	EAST
1 ♣	1 ◇
1 ♡	3 ♡
3 ♠	4 ♣
6 ♡	Pass

Result—six hearts bid and made.

East first makes the negative response of one diamond. He is then fully justified in jumping to three hearts on the second round of bidding—the same bid he should make with no score. While this is a mild slam try with 40 on score, East has already indicated the limited strength of his hand, so may bid aggressively without fear of deceiving partner. And his slam try can be made one level lower than in Standard American.

West might well take the plunge to six hearts immediately. However, if he wishes to be conservative he can make the cue bid of three spades. When East now shows his club suit West should need no further urging.

Some advocates of the standard method contend that even when opener's partner cannot keep the bidding open, the opponents may be afraid to enter the auction, for fear opener has an extra strong hand. But being passed out at the one-level is not always a good result. I recall this hand from one of the Italian-American World Championship matches:

WEST	EAST
♠ A J 10 x	♠ 9 xxx
♡ K xxxx	♡ ————
◇ A K Q x	◇ xxx
♣ ————	♣ Q J xxxx

The United States player sitting West made the "normal" opening bid of one heart. The other three players passed, and the contract was set one trick.

The Roman players who held these hands have a special convention to cover hands with three suits. They earned the admiration of the bridge world by bidding and making a four spade contract.

In Standard American there is no way to solve this particular dilemma. West does not have a hand worth forcing to game, and poor East is too weak to bid at all.

There would be little difficulty in getting to game using the Schenken System. The bidding would go:

WEST	EAST
1 ♣	1 ◇
1 ♡	2 ♣
2 ♠	3 ♠
4 ♠	Pass

East's second-round bid of two clubs is made simply to get partner out of a poor contract. If West now bids two notrump, East bids three clubs, a signoff.

However, West bids two spades, *not forcing* (planning next to bid three diamonds), and East's hand now takes on enough value to offer a raise. West pushes on to game.

One final hand showing how that pesky one bid can bedevil even expert players. This occurred in the 1960 intercity team-of-four match played between New York and Los Angeles.

WEST	EAST
♠ 4 2	♠ A 10 8 7 6
♡ A J 4	♡ 9 7 5
◇ A K Q 10 5 2	◇ 7 6
♣ Q 7	♣ A 10 4

For New York, experts John Crawford and B. Jay Becker

were East-West; for Los Angeles, Ivan Erdos and Ira Rubin. At both tables the bidding was:

WEST	EAST
1 ◇	1 ♠
2 ◇	Pass

The only way East-West could have reached three notrump was for West to bid three diamonds on the second round, an overbid according to these experts, for in Standard American the jump could be a much stronger hand. In my system the ranges are narrower, and I consider the hand clearly strong enough for my one club opening. Our bidding would be:

WEST	EAST
1 ♣	1 ♠
2 ◇	2 NT
3 NT	Pass

With two aces East makes a positive response, and the partnership is committed to a game contract. In this case three notrump is obvious.

Summary

All of the hands described in the chapter were played by nationally recognized experts. The poor results they obtained were in almost all cases not their fault, but the fault of the system they played. Had they used one club to show a strong opening bid I am confident they would have arrived at the best contract on all the hands I related.

4: *The One Notrump Opening*

Before continuing the treatment of the one club opening, I will digress to discuss the one notrump opening. This is similar to standard, showing 16 to 18 points, with a balanced hand of 4-3-3-3 or 4-4-3-2 distribution, and no suit weaker than three small or Q-x. It is also permissible to bid one notrump with a five-card minor suit.

♠ xxx   ♡ A Q 10   ◊ K J xx   ♣ A Q x   16 pts.

Bid one notrump.

♠ xx   ♡ A Q 10 x   ◊ K J xx   ♣ A Q x   16 pts.

Bid one heart. Many players today bid one notrump whenever they have 16 points, but I believe this is unsound practice with a worthless doubleton.

♠ Q 10 x   ♡ A K x   ◊ K Q x   ♣ K J xx   18 pts.

Bid one notrump. This is a maximum.

♠ A 10 x   ♡ A Q x   ◊ A 10 xx   ♣ A xx   18 pts.

Bid one club. When you add 1 point for all four aces, this hand is too strong for one notrump.

♠ K Q J 10   ♡ A 10 9   ◊ A 9 8   ♣ A 10 3   18 pts.

Another exception. Bid one club. You have six sure tricks.

♠ A x   ♡ K 10 x   ◇ K Q J xx   ♣ Q 10 x   15 pts.

Bid one notrump. The good five-card minor is worth at least 1 extra point.

Stayman After One Notrump

Used by almost every good player, the Stayman convention should become a part of your bidding equipment. The mechanics are simple. If over your opening bid of one notrump partner bids two clubs, he is requesting you to show a four-card major suit. With two four-card majors bid two spades. With no four-card major (or one weaker than Q-x-x-x or J-10-x-x) bid two diamonds.

The objective of the two club response is to find a contract better than notrump. Responder's distribution should indicate whether this is likely. Some examples will clarify this:

♠ K J xx   ♡ Q 10 xx   ◇ xx   ♣ A xx   10 pts.

Respond two clubs. If partner rebids in either major, jump to game. If his rebid is two diamonds, bid three notrump. You have at least 26 points in the combined hands, enough for nine tricks at notrump or ten tricks in a four-four major fit.

♠ K J xx   ♡ K xx   ◇ K xx   ♣ J xx   11 pts.

Respond three notrump. Even if partner has four spades, with this distribution it is preferable to play for nine tricks at notrump than ten at spades.

♠ J xx   ♡ Q 10 xx   ◇ J 10 xxx   ♣ x   4 pts.

Respond two clubs. Here you wish to get out of a hopeless one notrump contract into two of any suit except clubs. At notrump your hand is almost trickless; at a suit contract it is worth at least two tricks. You can use Stayman on such a weak hand *only* if you are prepared to pass any rebid by partner. Any second bid other than three clubs would be a game try.

♠ xx   ♡ xx   ◇ Q xx   ♣ Q 10 xxxx   4 pts.

Respond two clubs, then rebid three clubs. This is how to sign off in clubs. Partner is expected to pass.

♠ Q 10 xxxx   ♡ xx   ◇ xxx   ♣ xx   2 pts.

Respond two spades. This is a weak response and partner should pass. One of the features of the Stayman convention is the negative response of two in *any suit* except clubs. If you have a strong hand you must make some other response.

♠ Q 10 xxxx   ♡ xxx   ◇ A x   ♣ xx   6 pts.

Respond two clubs. If partner's rebid is two spades, raise to three. If his rebid is two diamonds or two hearts, bid two spades. This is the *non-forcing* variation of the Stayman convention. What it says in effect is this: "Partner, I do not have a bust but neither do I have enough to force to game. You may bid again if you wish, but with a minimum you are free to pass."

♠ Q 10 xxx   ♡ A xx   ◇ xx   ♣ xxx   6 pts.

Pass. Game is remote, and you have just as good a chance of making seven tricks at notrump as eight at spades.

♠ Q 10 xxxx   ♡ K xx   ◇ A x   ♣ xx   9 pts.

Bid three spades. No point to Stayman here. You wish to get to game and are leaving the choice between spades and notrump to partner.

♠ Q 10 xxxxx   ♡ xxx   ◇ A x   ♣ x   6 pts.

Bid four spades. This is a signoff bid—partner must pass.

5: *Stayman After One Club*

One of the features of the Schenken System is the use of the Stayman convention by either partner in auctions beginning with a one club bid. With a balanced hand opener will usually rebid notrump over a negative one diamond response, rather than show a four-card major. Responder can then use Stayman to find a major-suit fit.

(1)

	OPENER	RESPONDER
	♠ A K xx	♠ 10 x
	♡ A Q xx	♡ K 10 xx
	◊ K x	◊ Q xxxx
	♣ K xx	♣ J x

	OPENER	RESPONDER
	1 ♣	1 ◊
	1 NT	2 ♣
	2 ♠	2 NT
	3 ♡	4 ♡
	Pass	

Opener's one notrump rebid shows 19–20 points (or a strong 18). Responder's two notrump invites game, and opener shows his other major.

[41]

(2)

	OPENER	RESPONDER
♠	A K x	♠ Q 10 xxx
♡	A K x	♡ J xxx
◇	K Q xx	◇ J xx
♣	Q J x	♣ x

OPENER	RESPONDER
1 ♣	1 ◇
2 NT	3 ♣
3 ◇	3 ♠
4 ♠	Pass

Opener's jump to two notrump shows 21 or 22 points. Responder bids three clubs, planning to raise three hearts to four. When opener shows no major, responder shows his own suit. (If a player bids a major after using Stayman, he must have at least a five-card suit.)

With the values for a positive response (9 or more points and at least 1½ honor tricks), responder can show a five-card or longer suit by bidding one heart or one spade, two clubs or two diamonds. With an unbalanced hand responder can bid a four-card major.

♠ x   ♡ A Q xx   ◇ K 10 xx   ♣ J xxx

Because of the singleton spade, the proper response to one club is one heart.

♠ A K Q x   ♡ xxx   ◇ xxx   ♣ xxx

Because of the concentration of strength in the four-card suit, one spade is the best response to one club.

With a balanced hand, responder usually bids one notrump with 9 to 11 points, two notrump with 12 to 14 points. Opener can then use Stayman.

(3)   OPENER   RESPONDER
                   ♠ A xx   ♠ K xx
                   ♡ A K J x   ♡ Q 10 xx
                   ◇ A Q xx   ◇ xx
                   ♣ Q x   ♣ A xxx

                    1 ♣   1 NT
                    2 ♣   2 ♡
                    4 ♡   Pass

Opener shows extra strength by jumping when already forced to game. But responder has already shown all his values.

(4)   OPENER   RESPONDER
                   ♠ A K J x   ♠ Q xx
                   ♡ Q J xx   ♡ A K xx
                   ◇ A Q x   ◇ K xx
                   ♣ xx   ♣ J xx

                    1 ♣   2 NT
                    3 ♣   3 ♡
                    4 ♡   Pass

Opener bid one club rather than one notrump because of his worthless doubleton club. Had responder bid one diamond, opener would have bid one spade, planning to show his hearts next. This is one of the exceptional cases in which opener's first rebid would be a four-card major.

When the Stayman convention fails to reveal a major-suit fit it is sometimes possible to explore game and slam possibilities in a minor suit. For example:

                     OPENER   RESPONDER
                   ♠ A xx   ♠ K x
                   ♡ K Q 10 x   ♡ A J x
                   ◇ A K xx   ◇ Q J 10 x
                   ♣ A x   ♣ xxxx

These two hands can make five notrump or six diamonds. How do you get to the top contract of six diamonds? I suggest the following bidding:

OPENER	RESPONDER
1 ♣ (1)	1 NT (2)
2 ♣ (3)	2 ◊ (4)
3 ◊ (5)	3 ♡ (6)
6 ◊ (7)	Pass

1. Opener's club bid is quite strong with 20 points, all in top cards.

2. Responder's one notrump bid is near maximum.

3. Asking for a four-card major. The above hand illustrates an interesting point: After an opening bid of one club you can find a fit in either a major or a minor suit by using the Stayman convention. This should lead to many more good slam contracts.

4. No four-card major.

5. Showing a strong diamond suit.

6. An ace cue bid as he has denied holding four hearts, supporting opener's diamonds by inference. If responder's diamonds were weaker or shorter he would sign off with three notrump.

7. With all top cards and the good fit in diamonds, six should easily be made.

Usually 33 points are needed to produce a slam unless a good five-card suit is available. Here the needed extra trick is produced simply by ruffing the third round of spades with a high trump.

6: *When the Opponents Interfere*

As the opening one club bid is artificial the opponents should, whenever possible, enter the auction before the opener has the opportunity to show his real suit (or suits). For example, they may make a jump overcall of two or more in an effort to disrupt the orderly development of the bidding.

To combat interference bidding we have devised the following tactics: If after partner's opening bid of one club your right-hand opponent overcalls at the *one*- or *two*-level, a double is "positive" and shows that you have the values for a positive response. A cue bid in the opponent's suit shows the ace or a void plus a positive response. Any other suit or notrump bid over the overcall denies the strength for a positive response.

PARTNER	OPPONENT	YOU
1 ♣	1 ♡	?

♠ A Q x   ♡ xx   ◊ K J xx   ♣ xxxx   10 pts.

Double. This "positive" double is for takeout, not for penalties. It simply tells partner that you have a positive response.

♠ A Q x   ♡ K J 10 9 x   ◊ xxx   ♣ xx   10 pts.

Pass if the opponents are vulnerable! Partner must bid again. If he doubles (for takeout) you can convert to penalties by passing. If he bids, you will of course drive to game. If the opponents are not vulnerable, you should double and then bid notrump.

♠ Q xx   ♡ K J 10   ◇ J 10 x   ♣ 10 xxx   7 pts.

Bid one notrump. This shows two stoppers in hearts and fair values, but denies a positive response.

♠ K J 10 xx   ♡ K x   ◇ xxx   ♣ xxx   7 pts.

Bid one spade. You have a fair hand but not a positive response.

♠ Q J 10 xxx   ♡ xx   ◇ xxx   ♣ xx   3 pts.

Pass. You would deceive partner by bidding one spade. You will have the chance to show spades later.

♠ K Q xx   ♡ A   ◇ Q xxx   ♣ J xxx   12 pts.

Bid two hearts. You have a positive response and fine support for any suit. Slam is in the offing.

While most players use a jump overcall to show strength, many now use it as a weak nuisance bid. Since you already know your partner has a strong hand you should be able to cope with it.

PARTNER	OPPONENT	YOU
1 ♣	2 ♠	?

♠ K J x   ♡ Q 10 x   ◇ Q 10 x   ♣ J xxx   9 pts.

Bid two notrump. You have two spade stoppers, but not enough honor tricks for a positive response.

♠ xx   ♡ A K x   ◇ K xxx   ♣ xxxx   10 pts.

Double—equivalent to a positive response.

♠ K Q 10 9 x   ♡ xx   ◇ xxx   ♣ xxx   5 pts.

Pass! Remember, after partner's one club opening you cannot double the opponents for penalties at one or two of a suit. In this case it is unfortunate; but partner is expected to bid again, and he may make a takeout double, which you can convert.

If the opponent's overcall is at the *three*-level or higher, a double is for business. However, a bid neither affirms nor denies the strength for a positive response.

PARTNER	OPPONENT	YOU
1 ♣	3 ♠	?

♠ xx   ♡ A Q J xxx   ◇ xx   ♣ Q xx   9 pts.

Bid four hearts. You have a very good suit, and should not allow yourself to be shut out. Even though partner has another chance to bid if you pass, he may have a difficult problem. As you are already at a game contract, partner does not have to bid over four hearts, nor do you particularly wish him to.

♠ xx   ♡ xx   ◇ K Q xxxx   ♣ Q xx   7 pts.

Pass. A bid of four diamonds with your broken suit would be unsound. Since you are not at game, partner cannot pass four diamonds; and you will be beyond a possible three notrump contract which partner may attempt if you pass.

If the opponent doubles one club, a redouble shows the strength for a positive response. However a bid over the double denies this strength.

PARTNER	OPPONENT	YOU
1 ♣	Double	?

♠ A xx   ♡ K xx   ◇ K xxx   ♣ xxx   10 pts.

Redouble. This is tantamount to a positive response to one club.

♠ xx   ♡ K Q xxx   ◇ xxx   ♣ xxx   5 pts.

Bid one heart. This is a cheap level to show your suit, and denies the strength for a positive response.

♠ A x   ♡ K Q xxx   ◇ xxx   ♣ xxx   9 pts.

Again redouble. Never make the same bid on a strong hand that you would on a weak hand.

♠ xx   ♡ K Q J xxx   ◇ xx   ♣ xxx   6 pts.

Bid two hearts. This means that you have a good long heart suit, but are too weak for a positive response. Similarly, a jump to three hearts would be proper if you had a seventh heart.

Summary

The foregoing tactics are most important and should be learned and thoroughly understood.

1. The following bids by responder denote a positive response (9 points or more) to partner's opening one club bid.
   a. A double of an overcall at the one- or two-level.
   b. A cue bid in the suit bid by the opponent.
   c. A redouble of the opponent's double.
2. A bid by responder over the opponent's overcall at the one- or two-level shows some values but denies the strength for a positive response.
3. After the opponent makes a jump overcall to the level of three or more:
   a. A double by responder is for business.
   b. A bid by responder neither denies nor affirms the necessary high cards for a positive response.

7: *The One Diamond, Heart, or Spade Opening*

These are the "bread-and-butter" bids of the Schenken System. Bids of one in these suits occur far more often than all the other opening bids combined.

The usual high-card range is 12 to 16 points. With fewer than 12 points, extra playing strength is needed for an opening bid. With more than 16 points a one club bid or a bid in notrump should be made.

Keep in mind that the point count is only a rough guide to the proper evaluation of a hand. What ultimately matters is the ability to win tricks. When opener has one or two long suits the point count loses significance.

All good bridge players know that the point count is itself improperly proportioned—that aces are undervalued in relation to kings and queens. To maintain that a king is three-fourths as valuable as an ace, or that two queens are its equal, is clearly absurd. It would be more nearly correct to value an ace as the equivalent of a king plus a queen.

This would give the ace a valuation of 5 points. Here the pendulum would swing in the other direction—the ace would become slightly overvalued. Actually the ace is worth about 4½ points, but since most people dislike fractions, the *status quo* has been maintained.

To correct for the obvious inaccuracy of the point count, a few adjustments are made. For example, 1 point is deducted for an aceless hand, while 1 point is added for a hand containing all four aces.

For notrump bidding the point count is simple and fairly accurate. With 26 high-card points in the combined hands, including *at least two aces*, three notrump is a good but by no means certain contract. With a combined holding of 33 points, a small slam at notrump is often a tempting proposition.

For suit contracts some authorities add distributional points for short suits. If you must use points for suit contracts, adding for long suits as opener gives a more accurate picture. Add 1 point for the fourth and fifth card of each suit and two points for every card over five. Also give extra credit for a two-suit hand or three biddable four-card suits; partner probably has support for one of your suits.

In the following discussion I will evaluate hands as I would at the table—by estimating playing tricks, with the high-card point count in the back of my mind.

Most flat hands with 12 points should be passed. A good five-card suit, a fair six-card suit, or three four-card suits add enough distributional strength to make some of the following 12-point hands biddable.

♠ A K xxx ♡ A xx ◇ xxx ♣ J x 4½ playing tricks

Bid one spade. The good five-card spade suit justifies an opening bid.

♠ K xxxx ♡ A xx ◇ A xx ♣ J x 4 playing tricks

Pass. Your spades are too weak, and you have no convenient rebid if partner bids two clubs.

♠ K xxxxx ♡ A xx ◇ A x ♣ J x 5 playing tricks

Bid one spade. The sixth spade makes the difference.

♠ x ♡ A J 10 x ◇ K Q xx ♣ Q 10 xx
4½ playing tricks

Bid one heart. I value this hand thus: 1½ tricks in hearts, one trick in diamonds, ½ trick in clubs, plus ½ trick for each four-card suit. Possibilities of a fit are an added asset.

♠ A xx   ♡ K xx   ◊ Q xxx   ♣ Q J x   3+ playing tricks

Pass. As there are no distributional features, you estimate the playing strength of this hand in notrump. It comes to one trick each in spades and clubs, ½ trick in hearts and ½+ trick in diamonds. Added together they come to three-plus playing tricks, and *you should have more than four playing tricks when you have a minimum number of points.*

Sometimes an 11-point hand is worth an opening bid. A very good six-card suit or a two-suiter is needed.

♠ K Q J 10 xx   ♡ xx   ◊ A J x   ♣ xx   6+ playing tricks

Bid one spade. With five sure tricks in spades and one trick plus in diamonds, it would be an error to pass this hand.

♠ K Q J xx   ♡ K Q 10 xx   ◊ xx   ♣ x   7 playing tricks

Bid one spade. If partner can support one of your suits you will have about seven playing tricks.

Occasionally even a 10-point hand should be opened. A good two-suit hand is needed, usually in the major suits.

♠ K J 10 xx   ♡ A Q 10 xx   ◊ xx   ♣ x   6 playing tricks

Bid one spade. You should open this hand because you may easily make game if partner has a few key cards that fit. If you failed to open, you could easily pass out a game or part-score.

♠ A Q 10 9 xx   ♡ xx   ◊ K J 10 x   ♣ x   6 playing tricks

Bid one spade. About as good as the previous hand.

Observe again that as the high-card strength of a hand decreases, the playing strength must increase to compensate for the lack of top cards. Some of the 10- and 11-point hands above should win six or more tricks. Notice also that all these minimum point-count hands contain strong suits, well bolstered with tens and nines. The suits almost always include three honors, often in sequence. Remove the *tens* from such hands and they become doubtful opening bids.

To sum up, it is good tactics to open hands with substantial playing strength, despite minimum point count. Partner can rely on you for two defensive tricks, but not more.

Hands with 13 high-card points should usually be opened. For example:

♠ K xx   ♡ A xx   ◇ Q J x   ♣ K 10 xx

Here you have a full king over an average hand (10 points). If you were to pass this hand and your partner in turn passed a hand of similar strength, you would probably be passing out a game, since the combined hands would contain 26 high-card points.

In Standard American the opening bid on this hand would be one club. In the Schenken System one club may be bid only on a strong hand, so this hand must be opened one diamond. Responder must allow for the possibility of a three-card suit. He should have at least four diamonds to raise to the two-level, and five diamonds to jump-raise to the three level.

♠ K xxx   ♡ K xxx   ◇ K Q   ♣ Q xx

Pass. Again you have 13 points, but this hand should be passed, for three reasons: (1) You have no convenient bid. (2) One point should be deducted for an aceless hand. (3) Your doubleton diamond is not worth a full 5 points.

With 14 points you have a full ace more than your share of high cards, and the bidding *must* be opened. Generally there will be no problem, but occasionally you may run into an awkward hand:

♠ Q xxx   ♡ A J x   ◇ K x   ♣ A xxx

Bid one spade. You may not bid one diamond with only a doubleton, and the hand is much too weak to bid one club or one notrump. By elimination you must therefore bid one spade, although you would naturally prefer a better suit. Any response by partner can be easily handled. If he bids one notrump or two spades, you pass. If he responds with two in a minor suit, you bid two notrump. If he bids two hearts, you raise to three. (Partner knows your hand is limited.) Finally, if his response is three spades, the preferred rebid is three notrump. This leaves the decision between game at spades or notrump up to partner.

♠ A xx   ♡ A xx   ◇ Q xxx   ♣ A xx   3½ + playing tricks

Bid one diamond. Previously I stated that a minimum (10- to 12-point) opening bid should have at least four-plus playing tricks, whereas this hand is ½ trick short. This may sound contradictory. However, a balanced hand of 13 or more points will combine with any high cards or long suit in partner's hand, so you do not need as much playing strength of your own. For example, partner might hold:

♠ K Q xxx   ♡ K xx   ◇ xx   ♣ xxx   8 pts.

With normal breaks, the combined hands will produce two spades or two notrump.

Hands of 15 points are near the top category of opening suit bids. If partner responds you will make a vigorous rebid.

♠ A K xxx   ♡ A J x   ◇ xx   ♣ K 10 x

Open one spade. If partner raises to two spades, try for game by bidding three spades. If his response is two hearts, jump to game in hearts. If the response is two diamonds, a rebid of two notrump is better than two spades because of your extra strength. If the response is two clubs, the best rebid is three clubs. You would raise one notrump to two, for partner might have 10 or 11 points.

With 16-point hands the opening bid is one notrump unless you have a singleton, or a doubleton weaker than Q-x.

♠ A Q x   ♡ K J x   ◇ A Q 10 xx   ♣ xx

Open one diamond. If partner responds in a major you raise to
three. If partner's response is either one notrump or two clubs
you bid three notrump.

Here is a hand from the 1962 Masters' Team-of-Four, which
shows how establishing an upper limit on the opening one bid
makes subsequent bidding easier:

SCHENKEN	LEVENTRITT
♠ A	♠ K xxxx
♡ J 10 9 8 xx	♡ K Q
◇ K 10 x	◇ J xx
♣ A K x	♣ xxx

Our bidding was:

SCHENKEN	LEVENTRITT
1 ♡	1 ♠
3 ♡	4 ♡
Pass	

With 15 points in high cards and a good six-card suit, my
hand was close to a one club opening. Therefore I made an aggressive (but non-forcing) rebid, and we easily reached the sound
game.

At the other table opener rebid only two hearts, because a
jump rebid in Standard American shows a much stronger hand.
His partner had a close decision, but passed and missed the game.

Limiting the maximum strength of the opening bid pays divi-
dends on the weaker hands also. Consider this hand:

♠ K Q 9 8 x   ♡ J 10 x   ◇ ——————   ♣ A xxxx

In Standard American, this hand is too weak to be opened.
When I saw the hand played at rubber bridge, the complete deal
was:

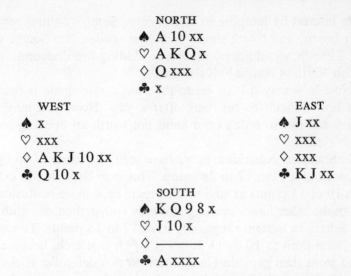

NORTH
♠ A 10 xx
♡ A K Q x
◊ Q xxx
♣ x

WEST
♠ x
♡ xxx
◊ A K J 10 xx
♣ Q 10 x

EAST
♠ J xx
♡ xxx
◊ xxx
♣ K J xx

SOUTH
♠ K Q 9 8 x
♡ J 10 x
◊ ———
♣ A xxxx

East was dealer; neither side vulnerable. The bidding was:

EAST	SOUTH	WEST	NORTH
Pass	Pass	3 ◊	Pass (1)
Pass	3 ♠	Pass	4 ♠ (2)
Pass	Pass	Pass	

1. North was stumped by the preempt. A double would be for takeout, and North was afraid his partner might bid clubs.

2. North had splendid support for spades, but the only slam try that would not take the hand above game was a cue bid of four diamonds, which North did not want to risk, holding no diamond control. So he took the conservative course, glad that his partner had found a reopening bid.

As the cards lay, seven was made by cashing three hearts, the ace of clubs, and nine spades by a crossruff. Seven is too much to bid, but six would easily have been reached had South opened the bidding one spade, as he would be able to playing the Schenken System.

West would overcall two diamonds, and North should show his

slam interest by jumping to three hearts. South's natural rebid is four hearts, and North simply bids four spades. But South, sensing a fine fit, should carry on by cue-bidding five diamonds, after which North of course bids six spades.

Note how easy it is to get to the slam if one spade is opened, and how difficult to get there after a pass. How, you may ask, can South bid so much on a hand not worth an opening bid in other systems?

In Standard American, as we have seen, the range of an opening one bid is from 12 to 24 points. This is so large that to extend it to 10 or 11 points as well would create even more confusion.

On the other hand, opening suit bids (other than one club) in the Schenken System range only from 12 to 16 points. To extend the lower limit to 10 or 11 points is no great stretch, because the hand must then provide (in addition to two defensive tricks) at least five-plus playing tricks. As he has the necessary playing strength—and the controls needed for slam—South can bid freely despite his meager point count.

Deal 65 from our victorious match against the French in Buenos Aires in 1961 illustrates further the aggressive tactics that can be employed when using limited opening suit bids.

NORTH
♠ K 5
♡ A Q 7 4 3
♢ Q 10 9 6
♣ 4 3

WEST
♠ A Q J 10 3
♡ J 10 5 2
♢ 5 4
♣ K 5

EAST
♠ 4 2
♡ 8
♢ K 7 3
♣ Q J 10 9 7 6 2

SOUTH
♠ 9 8 7 6
♡ K 9 6
♢ A J 8 2
♣ A 8

Neither side was vulnerable, and North was dealer. Our bidding was:

NORTH (Schenken)	EAST (Ghestem)	SOUTH (Leventritt)	WEST (Deruy)
1 ♡	2 ♣	2 ◇	2 ♠
3 ◇	Pass	3 ♡	Pass
4 ♡	Pass	Pass	Pass

Though a shaded opening, my hand took on added strength as the bidding continued. First, partner's two diamond bid fit my hand perfectly. Second, my spade king, behind Deruy's two spade bid, became almost worth an ace. Finally, partner's indication of heart support assured a fine fit in two suits.

I was only moderately lucky to make the hand. The spade king came through as expected, and the diamond king was on-side. But the hearts did not break, so I made 420 points.

At the other table, Trezel, though normally an aggressive bidder, elected to pass the rock-bottom minimum hand that I opened, and the bidding went:

NORTH (Trezel)	EAST (Silodor)	SOUTH (Le Dentu)	WEST (Kay)
Pass	3 ♣	Pass	Pass
3 ♡	Pass	Pass	Pass

When Silodor (playing Standard American) preempted three clubs, Trezel backed in with three hearts. Le Dentu, remembering his partner's original pass, chose the conservative course and passed, missing game. They scored 170 points, so our net gain was 250 points.

Deal 74 from the same match demonstrates an ancient and honorable principle of sound bidding—raise partner's suit if possible rather than rebid your own.

```
                          NORTH
                        ♠ Q J 7 5 3
                        ♡ K
                        ◇ J 7 4 3
                        ♣ K 8 5
        WEST                                    EAST
      ♠ 8 2                                   ♠ K 9 4
      ♡ J 9 4                                 ♡ Q 8 5
      ◇ 9 8 6 5 2                             ◇ A Q 10
      ♣ A J 7                                 ♣ 9 6 3 2
                          SOUTH
                        ♠ A 10 6
                        ♡ A 10 7 6 3 2
                        ◇ K
                        ♣ Q 10 4
```

Both sides were vulnerable; East was dealer. The bidding in
the other room was:

EAST	SOUTH	WEST	NORTH
(Silodor)	(Le Dentu)	(Kay)	(Trezel)
Pass	1 ♡	Pass	1 ♠
Pass	2 ♡	Pass	Pass
Pass			

I think that Le Dentu used poor judgment in rebidding his
shaky heart suit instead of raising spades. With scanty values and
an apparent misfit, Trezel passed, quite properly in my opinion.
South made five hearts, for plus 200 points.

At our table the bidding went:

EAST	SOUTH	WEST	NORTH
(Ghestem)	(Leventritt)	(Deruy)	(Schenken)
Pass	1 ♡	Pass	1 ♠
Pass	2 ♠	Pass	3 ♠
Pass	4 ♠	Pass	Pass
Pass			

When Leventritt raised my spades, my hand improved markedly, and I raised to three. Because his hand was already limited by his failure to open one club, Leventritt felt he had enough to contract for game. I played safe for four spades, and made plus 620 points, for a net gain of 420 points.

8: *Getting to the Best Contract After One of a Suit*

Here the simplicity of the Schenken System manifests itself. Because the range of opener's hand is so sharply limited, partner has far fewer problems than he would have playing other American systems.

You do not have to give opener a chance, wistfully hoping for that occasional "rock crusher." Opener may have a fairly good hand but cannot have a mammoth hand.

This being the case, partner can pass holding up to 8 points if he thinks that game is unlikely. For example, with:

♠ xxx   ♡ K xx   ◇ Q 10 xx   ♣ K xx

partner may pass an opening bid of one in a major. If the opponents reopen the bidding, you can then raise the major suit to two as a competitive bid.

In other systems, when opener's partner has to pass the opening suit bid he obviously has nothing. In the Schenken System this is not so, and sometimes an unlucky opponent can be trapped!

♠ 10 x   ♡ Q J x   ◇ K 10 9 x   ♣ Q 10 9 x

Suppose the opponents are vulnerable. Your partner opens one spade, and the next player passes. You pass because game is remote and there is a chance to win a large penalty. Your left-hand opponent reopens with two clubs or two diamonds, which is passed around to you. You should double with the expectation of setting him at least two tricks.

While this is a dividend that the Schenken System pays, the primary purpose is accurate bidding. By limiting opening suit bids you frequently play a hand at a low level and make a partscore, when others might go down at the three- or four-level.

Any response to an opening suit bid is at least partly constructive. A single raise should provide three to four supporting tricks, a double raise 4½ to 5 tricks.

Trump honors, and honor tricks in side suits, are what really count; but the point count can be used as a rough guide. Counting a doubleton as 1 point, a singleton as 3 points, and a void as 5 points, a single raise shows about 8 to 11 points, a double raise about 12 or 13 points including at least four trumps. Holding 11 or 12 points you do not have to invent a "temporizing" bid, as you would playing Standard American.

The choice between the single and jump raise is sometimes a matter of judgment. Holding:

♠ Q xxx   ♡ xx   ◊ K xxxx   ♣ A x

I would raise one spade to only two. But holding:

♠ Q xxx   ♡ xx   ◊ A K xxx   ♣ xx

I would raise to three. In the first hand the diamond king is a doubtful value. But the high cards of the second hand all have positive value.

The Jump to Game in Partner's Major Suit

A jump to three is invitational but not forcing (as in Standard American). If you wish to get to game either because of preemptive tactics or because you think you can make it (but not slam), you simply bid it. Three examples:

♠ A Q xxx   ♡ K xxxx   ◇ xx   ♣ x

♠ Q J xx   ♡ xxx   ◇ A Q xxx   ♣ x

♠ Q J xxx   ♡ x   ◇ K J xxx   ♣ xx

Partner opens one spade. With all three hands, jump to four spades. With the first two hands you expect to make game, but a slam is most unlikely. With the last hand you are preempting and will probably be set. However you are so weak defensively that you wish to make it as difficult as possible for the opponents to enter the auction.

In other systems, the jump to game in partner's suit is always preemptive. In the Schenken System you often have a good hand but no interest in slam, and expect to make the game. Your opponents have to guess. They may double with disastrous results, or bid and run into trouble.

On the following hand, deal 43 of our match against the French, we made a small but significant gain because of the preemptive effect of the direct jump to game on a good hand.

NORTH
♠ A 9 8 6
♡ 10 9 6 3
◇ 3
♣ A 8 5 2

WEST
♠ K 7 5 2
♡ K 4
◇ K J 10 5
♣ 9 7 6

EAST
♠ 4
♡ Q 8 2
◇ A Q 9 7 6 4 2
♣ J 3

SOUTH
♠ Q J 10 3
♡ A J 7 5
◇ 8
♣ K Q 10 4

Neither side was vulnerable; South was dealer. Our bidding was very direct:

SOUTH	WEST	NORTH	EAST
(Leventritt)	(Bacherich)	(Schenken)	(Ghestem)
1 ♠	Pass	4 ♠	Pass
Pass	Pass		

East's first chance to bid diamonds was at the five level, and he naturally was reluctant to come in. Deprived of the knowledge that his partner had a diamond suit, West failed to find the best defense—repeated diamond leads—and we made eleven tricks with ease, for plus 450 points.

At the other table, the bidding was:

SOUTH	WEST	NORTH	EAST
(Le Dentu)	(Kay)	(Trezel)	(Silodor)
1 ♠	Pass	2 ♣	2 ◇
3 ♣	4 ◇	4 ♠	5 ◇
Pass	Pass	Double	Pass
Pass	Pass		

Our teammates had no trouble finding the sacrifice, and went down two tricks, for minus 300 points. We gained 150 points.

The One-Over-One Response

In the Schenken System the only one-over-one responses are one spade or one heart over one diamond, and one spade over one heart. The usual minimum is 9 points in high cards. With a good five-card suit you may shade this to 7 or 8 points. Some examples, partner having opened one diamond:

♠ K Q 10 x   ♡ A x x   ◇ x x x   ♣ x x x   9 pts.

Respond one spade. As game is remote you will pass any minimum rebid by partner. If he rebids two clubs do not bid two diamonds, for he undoubtedly has at least as many clubs as diamonds.

♠ xxx   ♡ K Q xxx   ◇ xx   ♣ K xx   8 pts.

Respond one heart.

♠ A Q J xxx   ♡ xx   ◇ xx   ♣ xxx   7 pts.

Respond one spade. While weaker in high cards this hand offers 4½ or 5 playing tricks. Game is still unlikely, hence you should rebid your suit at the minimum level necessary.

♠ A K 10 xx   ♡ A K xx   ◇ xx   ♣ xx   14 pts.

Respond one spade, but make a jump rebid on the second round. Game must be reached.

The Two-Over-One Response

The response of two in a lower-ranking suit, as in other systems, usually shows 10 or more points. However, I believe it advantageous to show a long suit even with fewer than 10 points, rather than bid one notrump which partner might pass. Therefore responder does not promise to bid again if opener makes a minimum rebid. If partner opens one spade and you hold:

♠ xx   ♡ A Q J 9 xx   ◇ xxx   ♣ xx   7 pts.

respond two hearts. If partner bids two spades, pass; if he bids two notrump or three in a minor, bid three hearts. This indicates exactly what you have—a good suit but a weak hand.

Notrump Responses

In the Schenken System the response of one notrump is constructive and is usually based on a balanced hand of 9 to 11 points.

♠ xx   ♡ K xxx   ◇ A xx   ♣ Q 10 xx   9 pts.

Partner opens one spade. Respond one notrump.

♠ J xx   ♡ xx   ◇ A K xx   ♣ Q 10 xx   10 pts.

Raise one spade to two. Over one heart bid one notrump.

♠ x   ♡ J 10 xx   ◇ K xxx   ♣ Q J xx   7 pts.

Partner opens one spade. Here you should shade the response of
one notrump, as you have an unpromising singleton in partner's
suit and the other three suits well stopped. This is a bedrock minimum and if you had another spade you would pass. In fact, you
are bidding merely to reach a better contract. If partner passes or
bids another suit you have succeeded.

♠ xxx   ♡ xxx   ◇ A K xx   ♣ K J x   11 pts.

Respond one notrump to one in a major. As this is a maximum
hand, raise to three if partner rebids his suit. In Standard this
hand calls for a "temporizing" response, followed by another bid
after partner's rebid. You could easily be overboard.

♠ 10 x   ♡ Q 10 xx   ◇ A K xx   ♣ Q J x   12 pts.

If partner opens one heart, raise to three, invitational but not
forcing. If the opening bid is one spade, respond two notrump.
This response also is not forcing, and shows 12 or 13 points. You
must have at least one stopper in each of the unbid suits but
should not have good spade support. As is the case with raising
partner's suit, there is no need for an awkward temporizing bid.

Game-Force Responses

With 14 points or more (the equivalent of a compulsory opening bid) some game contract must be reached. Remember that
a jump raise or a jump to two notrump is not forcing. However,
any suit takeout by an unpassed hand is forcing for one round.

♠ Q x   ♡ A Q xx   ◇ K J 10   ♣ Q 10 xx   14 pts.

♠ J xx   ♡ K Q 10   ◇ A Q x   ♣ K 10 xx   15 pts.

If partner opens one spade, respond three notrump. This is not a slam invitation—it simply means that you expect to make game.

With the first hand, raise a one heart opening to four hearts. With the second hand, over one heart respond two clubs, a one-round force. Depending upon partner's rebid, contract for game in hearts or notrump on the second round.

Summary of Responses to Opening Suit Bids

Narrow-Range Bids

1. Raise to two of partner's major with at least three trumps and 8 to 11 points.

2. Jump to three of partner's major with at least four trumps and 12 or 13 points. This response can be passed.

3. Bid one notrump with a balanced hand and 9 to 11 points. Shade to 7 or 8 points only with a singleton in partner's suit.

4. Bid two notrump with a balanced hand and 12 or 13 points (not forcing).

5. Bid three notrump with a balanced hand and 14 or 15 points.

Wider-Range Bids

1. Bid one-over-one with 9 or more points. Shade to 7 or 8 points with a good five-card or longer suit.

2. Bid two in a lower-ranking suit with 10 or more points. Shade to 7 to 9 points with a good six-card or longer suit.

3. Make a jump suit takeout with 16 or more points; also with somewhat less when you have extra strong support for partner's suit, a very good suit of your own, or both.

9: *Nineteen Points:* *the Problem Number*

All followers of the point count know that a hand containing 19 points (or 20) is in the "twilight zone"—too strong for one notrump, but too weak for two notrump.

In standard bidding this is "solved" by opening with one of a suit; then, if partner responds with one of another suit, jumping to two notrump. If partner's response is one notrump, opener raises to two or three notrump.

This apparently solves the problem but there are often complications. Here are some:

Partner may be too weak to respond. Partner may also be short in your suit, in which case you are in a poor contract.

	EXAMPLES					OPENING BID
	Spades ♠	*Hearts* ♡	*Diamonds* ◇	*Clubs* ♣	*(Points)*	
(a)	A xxx	A K x	K J x	A 10 x	(19)	One Club
(b)	K xxxx	A K J	A K Q	xx	(20)	One Spade
(c)	A K Q x	K Q xxx	A J	xx	(19)	One Heart

Let us examine hand A. One club is the easiest bid to respond to and any response to this hand is satisfactory. However, if partner cannot find a response, the opponents have an option to bid if they wish, or to pass if they like clubs.

Now look at hand B. If partner cannot respond you may be set in this contract and yet be able to make a part score or even a game in another suit. Even if he can find a response of one no-trump, you may land in the wrong contract.

Partner might hold:

♠ x ♡ 10 xxxxx ◇ xxx ♣ A xx

or

♠ x ♡ xx ◇ J xxxxx ♣ A xxx

While it is a somewhat doubtful proposition, let us assume that partner responds with one notrump on both hands. What is your rebid?

To me three notrump is both obvious and imperative. Partner will surely pass and there you are in a frightful contract. Meanwhile you are probably missing games in hearts and diamonds respectively.

With hand C you will be in a good position if partner responds, since you can then show your spades, but suppose he holds:

♠ J xxxx ♡ xx ◇ Q xx ♣ xxx

Will he bid with three points? Very doubtful.

Reflect now what will happen if you open these problem hands with the forcing bid of one club. In all three cases the problem dissolves and you can get to the best contract with ease.

The 19-Point Slam Invitation

When auction bridge evolved into contract bridge back in the Roaring Twenties the bidding at first was simple "mama-papa" stuff. With three honor tricks you opened the bidding. With a like number of honor tricks responder made a jump response and then you bid for game. You also probably made it, since an opening bid opposite an opening bid will usually produce a game.

As the game developed and became more scientific, the opening bid remained the same but the requirements for a jump response in a suit became stronger and stronger.

The original reason for this, "not to crowd the bidding," makes a good deal of sense, but for the last ten or twelve years it has been fixed by bridge authorities at 19 points!

I know that in their lessons and writings bridge teachers and writers lean toward the ultraconservative. If you bid a slam and get set it is not going to be their fault. But 19 points to justify a jump response?

If your partner opens the bidding and you hold 19 points in high cards or even a little of it in favorable distribution, you have almost a sure small slam. You make your jump response, wind up at a slam, make it four times out of five, and your partner is duly gratified.

In other words the immediate jump response is forcing to a slam!

This is fine when you get the 19-point responding hand, but how often do you get it? When you do, can't you simply bid the slam yourself after finding out the best suit to play it in? Why must you have an almost sure slam to make a jump response? There are many responding hands of 15, 16, or 17 points you might hold where slam is possible but not certain.

With these hands, if you do not make a jump response on the first round you must make a strong jump bid on the second round. If you jump on the first round you can stop at game. Conversely, if you jump on round two you may land at four notrump or five in a major. If you are set a trick at such a contract you have tossed away a game.

When you believe the combined hands fit and slam is possible, is it not logical to issue your slam invitation at the first opportunity?

Assume partner opens with one spade and you hold:

	Spades ♠	*Hearts* ♡	*Diamonds* ◇	*Clubs* ♣	(High Card Points)
(1)	Q xxx	x	A K J xx	A xx	14 HCP
(2)	K x	A K Q J xx	K xx	xx	16 HCP
(3)	Q 10 x	x	A K Q xx	A xxx	15 HCP
(4)	K J x	xxx	A 10 x	A K Q x	17 HCP

None of these hands would meet the 19-point requirement of most of today's bridge writers. The singleton heart in hands one and three adds 3 points in distribution.

Hand two contains a solid suit with 7 playing tricks.

Hand four is an opening one notrump bid.

All four are sure game hands with slam possibilities.

This is the bidding I would recommend:

Hand 1.	OPENER	RESPONDER
	1 Spade	3 Diamonds
	3 Notrump or 3 Spades	4 Spades

Hand 2.	OPENER	RESPONDER
	1 Spade	3 Hearts
	3 Spades or 3 Notrump	4 Hearts

Hand 3.	OPENER	RESPONDER
	1 Spade	3 Diamonds
(a)	3 Spades	4 Spades
(b)	3 Notrump	Pass

Hand 4.	OPENER	RESPONDER
	1 Spade	3 Clubs
(a)	3 Spades	4 Spades
(b)	3 Notrump	Pass
(c)	3 Diamonds or 3 Hearts	4 Spades

With all of the above hands any bidding beyond game is left to the opening bidder. He is free to pass, but with some extra values or a good fitting hand he is equally free to bid for slam or make a further effort toward it.

To Summarize:

The 19-point jump response is another rut in which standard bidding has become bogged down. The slam invitational response should be just what the name implies—*not a slam force.*

10: *The Two Club Opening*

You may well have wondered what to open on a minimum hand containing a five- or six-card club suit.

The Italians use the opening bid of one notrump to describe a hand containing a club suit. This deprives them of the natural opening bid of one notrump to show a balanced hand of 16 to 18 points. In my opinion this is a serious flaw in their system.

In the Schenken System, a two club opening simply takes the place of a one club bid in other systems. The requirements are any six- or seven-card suit or a good five-card suit, and a point count of 11 to 15. The hand should not be strong enough for a forcing one club bid or an opening bid of three clubs (to be discussed in the next chapter).

Thus the opening bid of two clubs is sharply limited, the same as the opening one bids in the other suits. It gives partner precise information on which to act according to his strength. The bid is *not* forcing.

♠ xx ♡ xxx ◇ K Q x ♣ A K J 10 x   13 pts.

Open two clubs.

♠ xx ♡ K J x ◇ A x ♣ A Q J xxx   15 pts.

Open two clubs. This is the upper limit. Change the club queen to the king, or the heart jack to the queen, and you should open one club.

♠ xx ♡ Q x ◇ K Q xx ♣ A Q xxx 13 pts.

Open one diamond. The club suit is poor and the hand is very close to minimum.

♠ xx ♡ A xx ◇ A Q x ♣ K J xxx 14 pts.

Same as the previous example—open one diamond. Partner must always be on the alert for a possible three-card diamond suit. One diamond is preferable to two clubs on such a weak club suit. Change the hand to:

♠ xx ♡ A xx ◇ A xx ♣ K Q J xx 14 pts.

and you should open two clubs.

♠ A K J x ♡ xx ◇ xx ♣ A Q 10 xx 14 pts.

Do not open two clubs on a five-card suit when you have a good four-card major. Open one spade, then rebid three clubs if partner responds two diamonds or two hearts. In other systems this shows a strong hand and is forcing, but *your* opening spade bid was limited, so you can force only by jumping in an unbid suit.

♠ xx ♡ A K Q x ◇ xx ♣ A K J xx 17 pts.

Open one club. Here by coincidence you have a club suit which you may show later.

From the above it should be apparent that when you have five clubs, you must exercise your judgment in the opening bid. You may elect to pass a minimum hand if faced with an awkward rebid. You may also decide to bid a three-card diamond suit or a four-card major in preference to a five-card club suit. After a little experience you should easily be able to decide what to bid. A two club opening is about the equivalent of a two club overcall, and the vulnerability may well be the deciding factor.

♠ J x ♡ A xx ◇ A x ♣ Q 10 9 xxx 11 pts.

You should open two clubs not vulnerable, or with both sides vulnerable. But you should pass if vulnerable and the opponents not. In this last case the advantage of opening the bidding would be offset by the possibility of incurring a penalty of 800 if partner's hand proved worthless.

Here is an example taken from the semi-finals of the Vanderbilt Cup team-of-four championship, played in Lexington, Kentucky, in March, 1962. The opponents were vulnerable and it was my deal. I held:

♠ J x   ♡ 10 x   ◇ xx   ♣ A K J 10 xxx   9 pts.

In view of the vulnerability I elected to open two clubs. This was partner's hand:

♠ 10 xxx   ♡ A J xx   ◇ A J x   ♣ Q x   12 pts.

In response to my two club bid my partner, Peter Leventritt, bid two notrump, showing a good hand with at least two clubs. As I had seven potential tricks for him, I raised to game, and we scored 400 points (300 for making a non-vulnerable game, plus 100 for nine tricks at notrump).

When our opponent, Ira Rubin, held my cards he (playing Standard American) considered the hand too weak to open one club, and too strong for a preemptive bid of three clubs. He passed, and subsequently played the hand in three clubs, which he made, scoring 110 points (60 for nine tricks at clubs plus 50 for a part-score; in tournaments, honors do not count).

According to Rubin's own statement, there was no logical way to arrive at three notrump. Naturally I disagree. I believe that if three notrump can be made without even a finesse some method should be devised to get there.

Was my opening bid of two clubs dangerous? Not if properly handled. Certainly I could offer at least six playing tricks for a club or notrump contract.

What about the requirement of two sure defensive tricks? With a seven-card suit it was quite possible that my hand might take only one trick. However, if partner had doubled the opponents at a low level, I would probably have taken out the double.

All things considered, I had more to gain than to lose, and some risks have to be taken in bridge as in life.

Responses to Two Clubs

Two clubs is not forcing, but partner has several courses of action open to him. I have found that after two clubs, it is most practical to play a simple takeout to two in another suit as non-forcing (unlike after opening bids of one diamond, heart, or spade). Opener is at liberty to rebid, but may elect to pass.

In order to ensure a rebid by opener, responder can force by bidding two notrump, or by jumping to three of another suit.

♠ xx ♡ J xxx ◇ A Q J xx ♣ xx

Not vulnerable, respond two diamonds. This is simply to indicate a good lead and another suit to compete in if partner has a fit. If you pass and your left-hand opponent bids two spades, you cannot afford to come in at the three-level.

♠ 10 xx ♡ K xx ◇ A xxxx ♣ Q J

Raise to three clubs. Your two club honors should solidify partner's suit. With your raise he may be able to try for game in notrump.

♠ K Q 10 9 xx ♡ A 10 xx ◇ x ♣ A x

Jump to three spades, forcing. This indicates a very good suit which partner may raise on two small. If partner's rebid is three notrump, pass. If he bids four clubs, raise to five.

♠ K xx ♡ A 10 xxxx ◇ xx ♣ Q x

Respond two hearts. Game is possible if partner has a heart fit. However, if he now bids two notrump or three clubs, you lack the values for another bid.

♠ J 10 xxxx ♡ xx ◇ xxx ♣ A x

Pass. A bid of two spades would permit partner to bid higher, and might cause him to make a losing lead against some contract by the opponents. It is better to pass and hope for a chance to back in with two spades.

Rebids by the Two Club Opener

As previously stated, opener is free to pass unless the response was two notrump or a jump response in another suit. In considering a rebid, opener should be guided by whether he has minimum (11 to 13) or maximum (14 or 15) point count.

Let's consider one of the earlier examples again.

♠ J x   ♡ A xx   ◇ A x   ♣ Q 10 9 xxx   11 pts.

You should open this hand two clubs unless vulnerable and the opponents not. Now if partner responds two spades or two diamonds, you should pass. If he responds two hearts, you should raise to three. And if he responds two notrump, you should sign off with three clubs.

Suppose you held instead:

♠ xx   ♡ K J x   ◇ A x   ♣ A Q J xxx   15 pts.

If partner responds two notrump this is an ultra-sound raise to three. Suppose partner responded two diamonds. While you could pass, this hand is much too inviting. With two small spades a rebid of two notrump would be unsound. On the other hand, a mere rebid of clubs would be too conservative. I prefer a bid of two hearts! Partner should allow for the possibility that this may be only a three-card suit and an attempt to arrive at game in notrump. He should treat this rebid as forcing.

This brings to mind a hand I held recently:

♠ xx   ♡ Q x   ◇ K Q x   ♣ A K J 10 xx   15 pts.

I opened two clubs, and my partner responded two hearts. This presented a problem. I had a maximum hand, but considered both two notrump or a raise in hearts unsound. Three clubs would not do the hand justice, so I elected to bid three diamonds. Partner held:

♠ J 9 xx ♡ A J xxx ◇ A x ♣ xx

My three diamond bid induced him to bid three notrump, and with a little luck he made it.

The above examples are somewhat extreme, but it is important to remember that if opener bids a second suit after opening with two clubs he is forcing responder to bid again, and he may have only a three-card suit.

11: *The Three Club Opening*

Suppose you dealt yourself one of these hands:

♠ K x   ♡ xx   ◇ xxx   ♣ A K Q J xx

♠ xx   ♡ xx   ◇ xx   ♣ A K Q xxxx

Playing Standard American, you would undoubtedly bid one club with the first hand. What about the second hand? Some might open three clubs. But most players consider a solid seven-card suit too strong for a three bid. So you would probably pass.

Should you open the first hand with a Schenken two club bid? You might, but suppose partner had a hand like:

♠ Q 10 xx   ♡ A J 10 x   ◇ K J xx   ♣ x   11 pts.

With a singleton club he would pass, for he could not possibly know that you had a solid suit. Yet opposite each of the above hands he would have a good play for three notrump.

I would open each hand three clubs. This bid shows specifically a suit headed by A-K-Q-10 or better, at least six cards long, and a hand offering 6½ or 7 playing tricks in a notrump contract.

You might well ask, "Isn't it better to play the opening three club bid as preemptive?" I have several answers to that. To begin with, I found that it is important to differentiate between different types of club hands. A very strong hand, such as:

♠ A x   ♡ K x   ◇ xx   ♣ A K Q J xxx

should be opened with the artificial bid of one club, as the hand is too strong for either two clubs or three clubs.

[79]

I have already explained our opening bid of two clubs for a weaker hand. But I believe it of great importance to tell partner of the difference between a hand containing an ordinary opening bid with a club suit and a hand with a long solid suit.

To come back to the preemptive aspect, three clubs with a very weak hand does not often constitute an effective shutout. But three clubs as we use it is both an invitation to three notrump and, in effect, a preemptive bid.

Look at the defensive aspects of the first two sample hands. The first hand has a reasonable amount of defensive strength, unless one of the opponents has a singleton club. With the second hand you cannot count on more than one defensive trick. Thus if partner has a bust, the opponents might easily make game or even slam.

Opening three bids in the other suits or higher bids in any suit are treated as preemptive, just as in other systems. Since you are all familiar with bids designed to shut out the opponents, discussion is unnecessary.

Responding to Three Clubs

The opening bid of three clubs is of course not forcing. However, it is highly invitational, for it promises a hand that will take 6½ or 7 tricks. Responder should venture three notrump with stoppers in at least two suits, and at least two tricks in top cards.

♠ K x ♡ A xxx ◇ K 10 xx ♣ xxx   10 pts.

Bid three notrump. A lead up to one of your kings will give you at least eight tricks.

♠ Q xx ♡ K J xx ◇ K xxx ♣ xx   9 pts.

Pass. With an aceless hand and only two kings, three notrump is highly improbable.

♠ x   ♡ A 10 xxx   ◇ A xxx   ♣ 10 xx   8 pts.

Bid five clubs. You should have good play for this, and also wish to shut out spades.

♠ x   ♡ 10 xxxx   ◇ A xxx   ♣ 10 xx   4 pts.

Pass if vulnerable. Not vulnerable, bid five clubs as a shutout. You should be set less than the value of the opponents' sure spade game.

♠ K x   ♡ A J xxxx   ◇ K xx   ♣ xx   11 pts.

Bid three notrump. Three clubs invites notrump, not a suit bid. A three heart bid would be forcing, but might drive you beyond three notrump.

PART II

♣

SLAM BIDDING

One of the factors contributing to the lack of success of players using standard methods is their haphazard technique in bidding slams. I believe the basic difficulty stems from the very elastic opening bid of one in a suit and equally elastic responses. It is my contention that using the Schenken System you will bid more good slams, and bid them with far more ease and assurance.

One reason for this is the greater variety of bids that inform partner *immediately* about a strong hand. Slam bidding usually starts with a strong opening bid or an immediate strong response.

12: *Getting to Slam After a One Bid*

After Opening One Notrump

Slam bidding after the strong opening bid of one notrump is relatively easy. Holding a balanced hand, you simply add your points to the minimum and maximum (16 to 18) that the opening bid shows.

♠ Q xx   ♡ K J xx   ◇ A xx   ♣ A K x   17 pts.

Bid six notrump. With 33 points there will usually be a reasonable play for slam.

♠ A 10 x   ♡ K xx   ◇ K Q J x   ♣ Q 10 x   15 pts.

Bid four notrump. Partner can pass or bid on, depending on the quality of his hand.

Two very good four-card suits are worth a point each. A good five-card suit is worth about 2 points, and you may be able to make a slam with only 31 points in high cards.

♠ A x   ♡ A xx   ◇ K Q J xx   ♣ 10 9 x   14 pts.

In response to one notrump bid three diamonds. If partner rebids three notrump, bid four notrump. Partner may pass, but is invited to go on. In my opinion the four notrump is natural, but many players would consider it Blackwood. Be sure to ask your partner his interpretation in advance.

A good six-card suit is worth four points, but with long suits we come to the matter of controls. I recommend the use of the

Gerber convention after opening bids in notrump only—usually a direct jump to four clubs. Partner rebids as follows:

Four diamonds shows *zero* or *four* aces (you can surely tell which).
Four hearts shows *one* ace.
Four spades shows *two* aces.
Four notrump shows *three* aces.

If responder learns that two aces are missing he may pass if he thinks he is in the right contract, or sign off with a bid of four notrump. Over one notrump, responder should bid four clubs holding:

♠ K x   ♡ K Q 10 xxx   ◇ A xx   ♣ K x   15 pts.

Assume that opener bids four hearts, showing only one ace. Responder would naturally pass. Opener might have a sound notrump with this hand:

♠ Q J 10   ♡ A J x   ◇ K Q J x   ♣ Q 10 x   16 pts.

If responder's long suit were a minor, after opener's four heart bid responder would bid four notrump. This is a signoff bid announcing that the opponents hold two aces.

Let's assume now that opener bids four spades in response to Gerber, showing two aces. Responder should now bid a slam, and my preference would be in hearts to prevent a lead through one of the kings.

Finally, let's assume opener's rebid is four notrump, showing all three missing aces. Responder can now use the Gerber convention to ask for kings, by bidding five clubs. Opener shows his kings in the same way he announced his aces, but at the five-level.

With responder's actual hand, opener can have only one king. I will assume he shows it by bidding five hearts.

Responder can now count twelve tricks—six in hearts, and the ace and king of the other three suits. Hence responder should take a slight chance and bid seven notrump. If by some malign fate he is unlucky enough to be set, he can blame me for it.

Summary

Slams are not hard to bid after a one notrump opening, provided:

(1) The notrumper is consistent, that is, he has a balanced hand in the 16-to-18-point range.

(2) Responder adds up the possible minimum and maximum points in the combined hands.

(3) When necessary, responder uses the Gerber convention to check for controls.

(4) The Stayman convention is used to look for a fit in a major suit.

After Opening One Diamond, Heart, or Spade

When the bidding is opened with one of the above suits, responder knows at once that opener's hand is limited. While occasionally a hand may be opened with 10 or 11 points in high cards, the normal range is 12 to 16 points. With this limited range kept firmly in mind, responder should be able to tell at once whether or not a slam is possible.

When responder wishes to invite a slam, he will often start by making a single jump takeout in a new suit. This was the method used by Peter Leventritt with me in the finals of the Team-of-Four in Minneapolis in August, 1962. Our hands were:

SCHENKEN	LEVENTRITT
♠ 10 9 x	♠ A K Q J xx
♡ K xx	♡ A xxx
◊ A K xxx	◊ ——————
♣ A x	♣ K 10 x

The bidding:

SCHENKEN	LEVENTRITT
1 ◊	2 ♠ (1)
3 ♠ (2)	4 ♡ (3)
5 ♣ (4)	6 ♣ (5)
6 ♡ (6)	7 ♠ (7)
Pass	

1. Forcing to game, showing slam interest.

2. The obvious bid with fair trump support.

3. A definite slam invitation. This is a forcing cue bid showing the ace of hearts.

4. Another cue bid, showing the club ace.

5. Showing the club king and interest in a grand slam, as small slam is already assured.

6. Showing the heart king and by inference the diamond ace, without which a grand slam would not seem attractive.

7. Peter knew we had solid trumps, plus the ace and king of both hearts and clubs. He also knew I had at least three spades and was sure to have a singleton or doubleton in either hearts or clubs.

Two hearts were discarded on my ace-king of diamonds, and by simply ruffing a club in dummy Peter won all thirteen tricks. When our opponents held our cards, they stopped at six spades.

Notice how freely I bid on this hand. After opening the bidding and then raising spades, I later showed both the ace of clubs and the king of hearts. My reasons were:

1. With 14 points, I had more than a minimum bid.

2. I had a good diamond suit which might be useful.

3. My points were all in aces and kings. I had in fact four controls, which are of great value for suit slams.

When discussing the requirements for the opening bid of one club I stated that as little as 14 points in high cards are enough when you have a strong two-suiter. Nevertheless it is sometimes better tactics to bid one of your suits rather than one club. The following hand from the same tournament illustrates this:

NORTH
♠ xxx
♡ x
◇ J 8 xx
♣ K J xxx

WEST
♠ A Q J xx
♡ K xx
◇ Q xx
♣ xx

EAST
♠ K 10 9 xx
♡ Q J x
◇ x
♣ Q 10 xx

SOUTH
♠ ———
♡ A 10 9 8 xx
◇ A K 10 9 x
♣ A x

North-South were vulnerable; South was dealer. The bidding:

SOUTH (Schenken)	WEST	NORTH (Leventritt)	EAST
1 ♡	1 ♠	Pass	3 ♠
4 ◇	4 ♠	5 ◇	Pass
6 ◇!	Pass	Pass	Pass

Leventritt knew I had at least ten cards in the red suits. Since I had bid up all by myself to four diamonds, vulnerable, I should not be hurt at five.

In this competitive auction I could not be sure I would make six diamonds, but it looked like a very good gamble. After all, partner had raised me to five diamonds, and while this was a defensive bid, he had to have good trump support. In six diamonds I lost only a trump trick.

The important point of this hand is my opening bid of one heart, when my hand was obviously strong enough to bid one club. The reason is in two words: No spades! Suppose I had opened one club. West would have overcalled one spade. My partner would have to pass and East, in order to make life difficult for me, would have preempted three or four spades.

Suppose he bid only three spades. I would then bid four hearts. As the cards were I would have made this, if allowed to play it. On the other hand if an opponent bid four spades I would have to guess what to do next. Even if I guessed right and bid five diamonds, I doubt that partner would have found the slam bid.

The moral of this hand is: Be very wary of using the artificial one club bid when you are short in spades and much of your strength is distributional. Otherwise the opponents may preempt in spades and make it difficult for you to describe your hand except at a very high level.

When you have 17 points or more in high cards in addition to your distributional values, there is less danger of preemptive tactics by the opponents. If they do preempt, you have a wider choice of action. You may double them for a sizable penalty, bid one of your suits, or cue-bid their suit to force partner to bid.

The Blackwood Convention

When you and your partner have a good fit and plenty of points, to bid or not to bid a slam may be simply a matter of aces. Here the Blackwood convention can be useful.

Suppose you open one heart on a maximum hand in the Schenken System, such as:

♠ x   ♡ K Q J xx   ◇ K Q 10 xx   ♣ A J   16 pts.

and your partner responds with three hearts, a limited raise inviting game. You are sure to make eleven tricks; the only question is whether you can make twelve. If partner has two aces it is very probable. A bid of four notrump by you is Blackwood and asks partner how many aces he has. He replies as follows:

Five clubs shows *zero* or *four* aces.
Five diamonds shows *one* ace.
Five hearts shows *two* aces.
Five spades shows *three* aces.

If partner's rebid shows one ace, sign off at five hearts. If partner shows two aces, bid six hearts. This contract should be made in all likelihood.

In the somewhat unlikely event that partner shows all three aces, bid seven hearts! There is only one hand with three aces he can have that was not worth driving to game:

♠ A xx   ♡ A xxx   ◊ A xx   ♣ xxx

You can reasonably expect to discard two clubs on your diamonds and ruff your club in dummy.

Following a four notrump Blackwood bid, if the same player can account for all the aces and wishes to find out about kings for a grand slam he bids five notrump. Partner is then required to show kings in the same manner as he previously showed aces.

After one of our limited opening suit bids, the Blackwood convention is more likely to be launched by responder than opener. For example, after a one spade opening responder holds:

♠ K J xxx   ♡ K Q J x   ◊ A K x   ♣ x

Note that responder himself has first- or second-round control in all suits. Opener cannot have a hand where five spades is in jeopardy.

Hence responder bids four notrump. If opener's rebid is five hearts (two aces), responder bids six spades. If opener shows three aces, responder should bid seven spades.

Many players seem unable to bid toward slam unless they use Blackwood. They abuse a convention that should be initiated *only* when these two questions can be answered:

1. Will five be safe if I get a disappointing answer?
2. After partner's response will I know what to do next?

Let's change responder's distribution, without reducing his high-card strength, to:

♠ K J xx   ♡ K Q J x   ◊ A K   ♣ xxx

If responder bids four notrump and opener replies five diamonds, can responder be sure five spades will be made? No, for opener might have:

♠ A Q 10 xx   ♡ xxx   ◊ Q J x   ♣ K J

Opener has a sound bid, and yet at five spades might lose two clubs and a heart.

Suppose opener showed two aces. You would have to guess what to do next. If you decide to bid five spades, opener *must* pass since you are in full charge. Yet he might hold:

♠ A Q 10 xx   ♡ 10 xxx   ◊ Q J x   ♣ A

and you would miss a slam in either hearts or spades.

Obviously you should have tried for a slam without endangering your sure game. Suppose over one spade you make a jump takeout of three hearts. This bid is forcing to game and shows *some* interest in slam. (In some systems it is practically forcing to a slam!) Over your three heart bid, opener would bid four hearts. You now bid four spades, still not beyond game. With his fit in hearts and singleton ace of clubs, opener would cue-bid that suit. You are now on safe ground. You can, if you wish, jump right to slam. If still cautious, bid five diamonds, and your partner should bid the slam.

Showing Distribution

Responder can sometimes invite a slam by gradually revealing a distributional fit. After a one spade opening he may hold:

♠ Q 10 xx   ♡ A xx   ◊ A Q J xx   ♣ x

Game in spades is assured and slam is possible. How best to invite the slam without getting beyond game?

Responder first bids two diamonds, a one-round force. Assume opener rebids two spades. Responder next bids three hearts. This is a "reverse" bid, since the normal way to show two suits is to bid the higher-ranking first. It is a white lie, because responder does not have a genuine heart suit and has no intention of playing the hand there. This reverse bid is again forcing, and shows a strong hand.

Over three hearts, assume opener bids three notrump. Responder at last raises spades to four. What has opener learned about responder's hand?

1. He probably has a five-card diamond suit.
2. He presumably has a four-card heart suit.
3. He surely has good three-card trump support.
4. Therefore he evidently is trying to show that he has no more than one club.
5. He is inviting a slam.

If opener had this hand:

♠ A K xxx   ♡ Q xx   ◇ 10 x   ♣ K Q x

he could tell his club strength is largely useless and that even five spades is unsafe. But opener might have this hand:

♠ A K J xx   ♡ K x   ◇ K x   ♣ J 10 xx

Here his long weak clubs combined with the two red kings are extremely valuable. He could accept the slam invitation. He might bid five diamonds, in which case responder would bid six spades. Or he could bid four notrump and ask responder to show aces.

If opener had a hand such as:

♠ A K xxx   ♡ xx   ◇ K xx   ♣ A xx

over four spades he should make the cue bid of five clubs. Responder will probably then bid six spades, and opener should bid seven, for he can count thirteen tricks: two solid five-card suits, two aces, and a club ruff.

Occasionally the opponents' bidding may disclose the same singleton that responder revealed in the last hand. The bidding might be:

OPENER	OPPONENT	RESPONDER	OPPONENT
1 ♡	2 ◇	3 ♡	4 ◇

Now suppose opener's hand was:

♠ A x   ♡ A K 10 9 x   ◇ xxx   ♣ K J x

He should visualize a likely singleton diamond in his partner's hand. With a strong opening bid and no wasted diamond honors, he should invite a slam by bidding four spades. If responder has:

♠ K J xx   ♡ Q xxx   ◇ x   ♣ A 10 xx

he will bid six hearts.

Finally we come to the direct leap to slam without revealing any high cards or distribution. It might come about when opener has bid one spade and responder's hand is:

♠ K 10 xxx   ♡ ——   ◇ A K J xxx   ♣ xx

A jump to six spades is unscientific but often effective. Opener may have a high club honor. If not, the opponent has to guess which of three suits to lead. You'd be surprised how often he will guess wrong.

After Opening One Club

An opening one club bid shows at least 17 points, although as many as three points of this may be in distribution. A positive response shows at least 9 points, except when responder has two bare aces, 8 points. Thus both partners know after the very first round that even if the club bid and the positive response are each minimum, a game must be reached. They know also that any extra strength in either hand will point toward slam.

My wife and I used this knowledge to good purpose in the National Mixed Team-of-Four in Minneapolis, when we arrived at a slam that very few pairs bid.

SCHENKEN	MRS. SCHENKEN
♠ A 10	♠ Q xx
♡ A J 9	♡ x
◇ 10 x	◇ A Q J xx
♣ A K Q xxx	♣ xxxx
1 ♣	2 ◇
3 ♣	4 ♣
6 ♣	Pass

Short, simple, and easy to get to. Yet the bidding at most tables went like this:

OPENER	RESPONDER
1 ♣	1 ◇
3 NT	Pass

Responder passed because he could not be sure opener had a real club suit, and therefore he was afraid to get beyond the game in notrump.

Although I happened to have a very strong club suit, my opening club bid was artificial. Bee had just about enough to make a positive response—9 points including 1½ honor tricks—and bid two diamonds, as one diamond would show weakness.

My three club bid showed a genuine suit. With four trumps and a singleton my wife's hand took on added value. When she raised my clubs to four, it was no feat on my part to bid the ironclad slam.

A Slam in Notrump

OPENER	RESPONDER
♠ xx	♠ A Q xx
♡ A K Q	♡ 10 xx
◇ A K xxx	◇ Q x
♣ A K J	♣ Q xxx
1 ♣	1 NT
6 NT	Pass

As I pointed out in Chapter 1, opener might bid one diamond playing Standard American. Responder would bid one spade. It would then be a matter of guesswork whether the slam was reached. In the Schenken System the bidding is short and sweet. The proper hand becomes declarer, protected against a possibly fatal spade lead.

With a Part-Score

The possession of a part-score costs players of Standard American thousands of points in slam bonuses. The already wide ranges of the bids become even wider, because either player might be stretching his hand to get to game.

I gave one illustration earlier, in Chapter 3. Here is another hand which I saw recently at the Cavendish Club.

OPENER	RESPONDER
♠ A Q 10	♠ K 9 xx
♡ K Q J 9 x	♡ A x
◇ A xx	◇ xx
♣ K x	♣ A Q 10 xx

This was the actual bidding, with 40 on score:

OPENER	RESPONDER
1 ♡	2 ♣
2 NT!	Pass!

Neither player was aware that the other had considerable extra strength. Both of them leaned over backward to avoid the embarrassment of bidding too high and going down. They were wrong, of course, but the fault lay in their tools more than in their technique.

I tested this hand on two average players who were familiar with the principles of my System, and they bid thus:

OPENER	RESPONDER
1 ♣	2 ♣
2 ♡	2 ♠
3 ♠	4 ♡
4 NT	5 ♡
5 NT	6 ◇
7 ♡	Pass

Simple, direct, and effective. Neither of them had to worry about getting too high, because in the first round of bidding the strength of each hand was identified—opener's by his one club bid, responder's by his positive response.

After Interference Bidding

The next example is a recent hand where a slam was reached after interference bidding by the opponents.

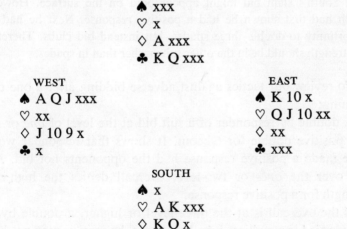

```
                          NORTH
                          ♠ xxx
                          ♡ x
                          ◇ A xxx
                          ♣ K Q xxx

      WEST                                    EAST
      ♠ A Q J xxx                             ♠ K 10 x
      ♡ xx                                    ♡ Q J 10 xx
      ◇ J 10 9 x                              ◇ xx
      ♣ x                                     ♣ xxx
                          SOUTH
                          ♠ x
                          ♡ A K xxx
                          ◇ K Q x
                          ♣ A J 10 x
```

South dealer; neither side vulnerable. The bidding:

SOUTH	WEST	NORTH	EAST
1 ♣	2 ♠ (1)	Double (2)	3 ♠ (3)
Pass (4)	Pass	4 ♣ (5)	Pass
6 ♣ (6)	Pass	Pass	Pass

1. A typical weak jump overcall.

2. The Schenken "positive" double. It simply means that if West had passed, North would have made a positive response. (Conversely, any bid by North would deny the values for a positive response.)

3. A further interference bid.

4. Since North may not pass three spades, South allowed the bid to come to him.

5. North was glad to show his club suit.

6. South's slam bid might appear bold on the surface. However North had first shown he had a positive response. Next he had the opportunity to double three spades, but instead bid clubs. Therefore his strength should be in the other suits rather than in spades.

To review our tactics against adverse bidding after a one club opening:

A double by responder of a suit bid at the level of *one* or *two* is a positive double for takeout. It shows that responder would have made a positive response had the opponents not bid. Any bid over the one- or two-level overcall denies the high-card strength for a positive response.

If the overcall is at the three-level or higher, a double by responder is for penalties. If he bids a suit, he may or may not have the high cards for a positive response.

After a Negative Response

OPENER		RESPONDER	
♠ A K xxx		♠ Q 10 xx	
♡ A 10 xx		♡ x	
◇ x		◇ A xxx	
♣ A Q 10		♣ J xxx	
1 ♣		1 ◇	
1 ♠		3 ♠ (1)	
4 ♣ (2)		4 ◇ (3)	
4 ♡ (4)		6 ♠ (5)	
Pass			

The first three bids are automatic. Opener has a sound one club bid with 17 points in high cards and two good suits. Responder must make the negative one diamond response, and opener's rebid of one spade is non-forcing.

1. However, responder has such a fine fit for spades that game is assured. His forcing jump to three spades is made with the hope that opener will make a slam try.

2. Opener obliges by bidding four clubs, a cue bid showing the ace.

3, 4. Responder's bid of four diamonds and opener's bid of four hearts are ace-showing.

5. In view of opener's two slam tries responder's hand has become of great value. He has four-card trump support, an ace, a club honor, and a vital singleton in hearts that should be worth at least two tricks. A good slam contract.

Using standard methods opener would bid one spade and responder can raise only to two. An expert pair might conceivably still arrive at the slam, but an average pair would not. I contend that the opening club bid makes the subsequent bidding much easier.

Showing Solid and Semi-Solid Suits

A self-sufficient suit is a valuable asset which should be capitalized on for slam. I have already discussed one way to show a solid suit—the opening bid of three clubs. Other ways to be discussed in the next chapters are the opening bids of two or three notrump and two diamonds. All these ways to show suits which do not need support from partner constitute a powerful factor in accurate slam bidding in the Schenken System.

There are easy ways to show strong suits after a one club bid also. As any response except one diamond commits the partnership to game, jump bids can be put to special use.

The general principle is this: *When a bid would be forcing, a jump to the next higher level shows a solid suit*—at least A-K-Q-J-x, A-K-Q-10-x-x, or A-K-Q-x-x-x-x. *A jump to the second higher level shows a semi-solid suit*—a suit needing only the ace, king, or queen from partner to be solid.

All these bids by responder show solid suits:

OPENER	RESPONDER
1 ♣	2 ♡, 2 ♠, 3 ♣, or 3 ◇

♠ K xx   ♡ A K Q J x   ◇ xxx   ♣ xx

Responder must have at least six potential playing tricks for this jump, hence at least one king on the side if he has only a five-card suit.

♠ A K Q 10 xx   ♡ xx   ◇ xx   ♣ J xx

♠ xx   ♡ xx   ◇ Q x   ♣ A K Q xxxx

♠ x   ♡ xxxx   ◇ A K Q J xx   ♣ xx

All these bids by responder show semi-solid suits:

OPENER   RESPONDER
1 ♣   3 ♡ , 3 ♠ , 4 ♣ , or 4 ◇

♠ x   ♡ A Q J 10 xx   ◇ K J x   ♣ xxx

♠ K Q J 10 xx   ♡ A xx   ◇ xx   ♣ xx

♠ x   ♡ Q x   ◇ A K x   ♣ K Q J 9 xxx

♠ xx   ♡ x   ◇ A Q J xxxx   ♣ A Q x

For any of these bids responder must have at least the 1½ honor tricks needed for a positive response. Note that the minor-suit hands tend to be very powerful both in high cards and playing strength, because the level is so high. Holding a weaker hand, responder need not exercise his option to show a semi-solid *minor* suit, but should make a simple positive response.

The following hand illustrates the simplicity of this method of bidding:

OPENER   RESPONDER
♠ A K xx   ♠ xx
♡ x   ♡ A K Q J xxx
◇ A K Q x   ◇ xx
♣ K xxx   ♣ xx

1 ♣   2 ♡ (1)
2 NT (2)   4 ♡ (3)
5 NT (4)   6 NT (5)
Pass

1. A positive response showing a solid suit.

2. Opener does not have a good long suit to bid. The hand must be played in hearts or notrump.

3. Responder shows six or seven absolutely solid hearts. He cannot have an outside ace, or he would not jump to game—a bid that might be passed.

4. Opener can see at least eleven tricks if he is declarer.

5. Responder realizes that opener wants the lead coming up to his hand, and with seven sure tricks he is ready to oblige.

Six notrump from the right side of the table is difficult to reach confidently without our method of showing solid suits.

If opener bids one club and gets a *positive* response, he too can show a solid or semi-solid suit according to the principle given above.

OPENER	RESPONDER
1 ♣	1 ♡
2 ♠, 3 ♣, or 3 ◇	

♠ A K Q J xx ♡ A x ◇ K xx ♣ xx

♠ A x ♡ K x ◇ A xxx ♣ A K Q J 10

♠ x ♡ xx ◇ A K Q xxxx ♣ A K x

OPENER	RESPONDER
1 ♣	1 NT
4 ♡	Pass

♠ A x ♡ K Q J 10 xx ◇ K x ♣ A xx

Responder may pass but holding 10–11 points should bid again. Note however that over a *negative* response of one diamond, a non-jump bid would not be forcing, so the single jump merely shows a forcing hand, not a solid suit.

13: *Optional Notrump Openings*

In the Schenken System balanced hands of 21 or 22 points are best described by opening the bidding one club. Assuming partner responds one diamond, opener then bids two notrump.

With a hand so strong in high cards, interference bidding by the opposition is welcome. And whenever partner is able to make a positive response to one club, you gain two distinct advantages:

1. When you have the 21- or 22-point hand you know immediately that a slam is possible.

2. You can exchange information as to high-card strength and distribution, starting at the one-level. You can investigate thoroughly all possibilities and decide at your leisure where to play the hand.

As two (or three) notrump openings are not needed to show balanced strong hands, these bids can be used to show strong notrump-type hands with a solid minor suit. Naturally they are stronger hands than those described by a three club opening, and include all suits stopped or potentially stopped. The requirements are:

>   For two notrump: 17 to 20 points, 7 or 8 playing tricks
>   For three notrump: 17 to 22 points, 8½ or 9 playing tricks

An ace, king, or queen in each side suit. The long minor suit must be at least as good as A-K-Q-J-x, A-K-Q-10-x-x, or A-K-Q-x-x-x-x.

    ♠ K x x   ♡ K x   ◇ A K Q J x ♣ K x x   19 pts.

While this hand might also be opened one club, I believe two notrump describes it better. A lead up to any of your kings gives you six sure tricks, and you will probably make another trick even if partner has a complete bust. If partner has as little as one bare ace, you may make game.

Incidentally, if partner's hand is worthless, the opponents can probably make a part-score and possibly even game in one of the major suits, and the two notrump bid may shut them out.

♠ Q 10 x ♡ K x ◇ K x ♣ A K Q 10 xx 17 pts.

This is a classic two notrump bid, with about eight potential playing tricks.

♠ Q x ♡ K x ◇ A K Q J xxx ♣ A x 19 pts.

Open three notrump! While I prefer to have all suits stopped, I would make an exception with this 8½-trick hand. With three short suits, spades may not necessarily be opened. If they are, let's hope partner has length or a stopper.

♠ A x ♡ A x ◇ K x ♣ A K J xxxx 19 pts.

Bid one club, because your suit is not solid.

♠ A J 10 ♡ K x ◇ A K Q J x ♣ A xx 22 pts.

Bid three notrump. You have seven fast tricks and two potential tricks. This hand has the maximum high-card holding for three notrump.

♠ A x ♡ A x ◇ A x ♣ A K Q J xxx 22 pts.

Open two diamonds (to be discussed later). With ten sure tricks, you can make a slam if you find partner with two kings or the king-queen of some suit.

Responses to Two Notrump Bids

The opening bid of two notrump is not forcing. You should have at least an ace, or a king and a queen, or three queens for a raise to three notrump. Expressed in points, from 4 to as many as 10 points.

Note that while comparatively little is needed to make game, quite a lot may be needed to produce a slam. With a balanced hand but no long suit, raise to four notrump with 11 or 12 points, to six with 13 or 14 points.

For an opening two or three notrump bid it is mandatory that the opening bidder have one high card (ace, king, or queen) in each side suit. Responder can then rely on this to bolster any good suit he may hold. Thus, hands such as:

♠ A xx   ♡ K Q J xx   ◇ xxx   ♣ xx

♠ A Q J xxx   ♡ xx   ◇ K xx   ♣ xx

♠ xx   ♡ A x   ◇ xx   ♣ K Q J xxxx

are worth respectively six, seven, and eight playing tricks, as opener must have the high card to solidify the long suit.

With these hands you have enough potential playing tricks to make six or seven. Remember partner has a long solid suit of his own, so it is unnecessary for you to show your suit. Also it is desirable for the lead to come up to partner's hand.

However, the opponents may still have two fast tricks—two aces, or the ace and king of some suit—against you. Therefore it is desirable to investigate how many controls there are in the combined hands. Responder can find out by using the Gerber convention, in this case by bidding *three* clubs.

The responses are similar to Gerber, but one level lower. Three hearts shows one ace; three spades shows two aces; three notrump shows three aces; and three diamonds shows all four. (Opener cannot be aceless, for he necessarily has the ace of his solid suit.)

If you subsequently wish to find out about kings, you bid four clubs, and partner responds in like fashion.

Let's pair up some of our sample hands and see how this works.

OPENER	RESPONDER
♠ K xx	♠ xx
♡ K x	♡ A xx
◇ A K Q J x	◇ xxx
♣ K xx	♣ A Q J xx
2 NT	3 ♣ (1)
3 ♡ (2)	4 ♣ (3)
4 ◇ (4)	6 NT (5)
Pass	

1. The Gerber convention, asking for aces.
2. Showing one ace.
3. Slam can still be made if opener has all the kings.
4, 5. Opener shows all four kings, hence twelve tricks are assured.

Note that with the opening bidder as declarer, the slam cannot be defeated; whereas if responder were declarer, a spade lead might be ruinous. Incidentally, if opener shows only three kings, responder should sign off with four notrump, which opener must pass.

OPENER	RESPONDER
♠ Q 10 x	♠ K x
♡ K x	♡ xx
◇ K x	◇ A Q 10 xxx
♣ A K Q 10 xx	♣ xxx
2 NT	3 ♣ (aces?)
3 ♡ (one ace)	3 NT (signing off)
Pass	

In considering responses to the opening bid of two notrump, responder should bear in mind that opener can usually win seven tricks without any assistance. Therefore rescue bids are unnecessary. There is also very little point in showing a five-card suit. It follows that a bid of three in one of the majors is forcing, and shows at least a six-card suit and distinct preference for suit play.

♠ Q J 10 xxx   ♡ xx   ◇ xx   ♣ xxx

Pass. A bid of three spades will land you at either three notrump or four spades. As you probably cannot make either contract, it is better to let partner struggle.

♠ Q J 10 xxx   ♡ Q xxx   ◇ xx   ♣ x

Bid three spades. Over three notrump, bid four spades. With this distribution you should have a better chance for game in spades than in notrump.

♠ A J 10 xxx   ♡ xxx   ◇ xxx   ♣ x

Bid three spades, but pass if partner bids three notrump.

♠ xx   ♡ A Q J xxx   ◇ Q xx   ♣ xx

Jump to four hearts. This is a mild slam try. Partner will pass unless he has high-card controls in all four suits, including two aces.

Responses to Three Notrump

When the opening bid is three notrump responder should pass unless he has a freakish hand that offers a better chance for game in his suit, or if he has slam possibilities.

♠ J 10 9 8 xxx   ♡ x   ◇ x   ♣ J xxx

Bid four spades. This is a signoff.

With a balanced hand responder may raise to four notrump with 9 or 10 points, to six notrump with 11 or 12 points. Usually it is preferable to use the Gerber convention (four clubs) to check on controls. For example:

OPENER	RESPONDER
♠ Q x	♠ A J x
♡ K x	♡ Q J 10 xx
◇ A K Q J xxx	◇ xx
♣ A x	♣ K xx
3 NT	4 ♣ (aces?)
4 ♠ (2 aces)	6 NT
Pass	

While the combined hands have at least 14 potential tricks, the opponents have an ace that must win a trick.

OPENER	RESPONDER
♠ A J 10	♠ xx
♡ K x	♡ A J xx
◇ A K Q J x	◇ 10 x
♣ A xx	♣ K Q J xx
3 NT	4 ♣ (aces?)
4 NT (3 aces)	5 ♣ (kings?)
5 ♠ (2 kings)	7 NT

Responder can easily count 13 tricks—two solid five-card suits and ace-king, ace on the side.

Summary

The Schenken System opening bids of two and three notrump give such precise and valuable information that they are practically foolproof for slam purposes, provided the following precautions are taken:

1. Opener's suit should always equal or exceed the requirements given.

2. Opener must have an ace, king, or queen in every suit.

3. Rather than jump to a slam, responder should use the Gerber convention to check on controls.

14: *The Two Diamond Opening*

The one club opening and the various notrump openings cover about 95 per cent of all strong hands. The rest are covered by the two diamond opening, which shows one of two types of hands: a balanced hand with 23 or more points, or a hand with a long strong suit, on which game is assured and slam depends on responder having specific honor cards *that fit opener's hand*.

The last four words are the key to the two diamond bid. By means of a comprehensive structure of artificial bids, responder can show exactly which high cards he holds. But he is not supposed to show his own suits.

If opener wants to find out about responder's distribution, he must open one club, not two diamonds. Suppose, for instance, you were dealt:

♠ A K Q 10 x   ♡ A K Q 10 x   ◇ A K   ♣ A

As partner's high cards are of no interest, you open one club. Over his one diamond response, you force with two spades. If he responds two notrump, you force again with three hearts. Partner's next bid should help you decide whether to bid six or seven hearts or spades.

When partner opens two diamonds, your first responsibility is to show what aces you hold, in the following manner:

1. With *no aces*, respond two hearts, the cheapest bid.
2. With *the heart ace*, respond two notrump. This avoids having to jump to three hearts to show that ace.

3. With the *spade, club, or diamond ace,* respond two spades, three clubs, or three diamonds respectively.

4. With *two aces,* jump in the suit of the higher ranking ace. Opener can then find out your second ace by repeating his *diamond* bid at the cheapest level. Slam is likely.

5. With *three aces,* double-jump in the suit of the highest ranking ace (that is, bid four hearts or four spades). Slam is assured, as partner had game without your aces.

Suppose responder bids two hearts, denying any aces, and opener bids two notrump. This shows an "in-between" hand of 23 to 25 points—too strong for one club followed by two notrump, yet too weak to insist on game. Responder can pass with a bust and no suit, bid a suit of his own, or raise notrump.

Holding 26 or 27 points, opener jumps to three notrump.

Showing Kings and Queens

Opener can quite often place the final contract after determining responder's aces. On occasion he will be interested in locating one or two vital kings. The method I have evolved for doing this is fairly easy to grasp. Nevertheless, it will come up so seldom that I recommend you use it only with a regular partner with whom you have discussed it in detail.

In this method, the *cheapest* bid by opener after the ace-showing answer to two diamonds asks responder to show his kings. If responder has no kings, he makes the *cheapest* response. If he has one or more kings, he shows them in the same way as he showed aces.

OPENER	RESPONDER
2 ◇ (aces?)	2 ♡ (no aces)
2 ♠ (kings?)	2 NT (no kings)

To show the spade king (and no other), responder bids three spades. To show two kings, responder jumps in the suit of the higher one.

OPENER	RESPONDER
2 ◇ (aces?)	2 NT (heart ace)
3 ♣ (kings?)	3 ◇ (no kings)

Responder's cheapest bid shows no kings. To show the diamond king (and no other) responder bids three notrump. A jump to four diamonds would show the diamond and club kings.

OPENER	RESPONDER
2 ◇ (aces?)	3 ♡ (heart ace and
3 ♠ (kings?)	one lower ace)

Opener apparently knows which is responder's second ace, for he did not ask by bidding four diamonds.

OPENER	RESPONDER
2 ◇ (aces?)	3 ♣ (club ace)
3 ◇ (kings?)	4 ♠ (spade king and one other king)
5 ◇ (which?)	6 ♣ (club king)

Opener must be sure of at least a small slam opposite the club king.

On rare occasions, after locating aces and kings, opener can ask for queens—again by making the *cheapest* rebid.

OPENER	RESPONDER
2 ◇ (aces?)	2 ♠ (spade ace)
2 NT (kings?)	3 ♣ (no kings)
3 ◇ (queens?)	

Responder bids as before—three hearts for no queen, three notrump for the heart queen, and a jump for two queens.

If opener does not make the cheapest rebid, he is no longer interested in high cards. However, he is still in command of the hand.

OPENER	RESPONDER
2 ◇ (aces?)	2 ♠ (spade ace)
3 ♠	

Opener's suit is spades, and responder bids naturally, except that he may not pass below game.

OPENER	RESPONDER
2 ◊ (aces?)	2 ♡ (no aces)
4 ♡	Must pass

To get the best results from this method, opener should always weigh the consequences of each of partner's responses before deciding to ask for honors of a particular rank.

Now let's see how this method works in practice.

♠ A Q 10   ♡ A Q x   ◊ A K x   ♣ A K J x   27 pts.

This phenomenal hand was dealt to my partner, Peter Leventritt, in the Vanderbilt Cup Team-of-Four. He opened two diamonds, and this was my charming hand:

♠ 9 xx   ♡ 9 8 xx   ◊ 9 xx   ♣ 9 xx

I of course responded two hearts. What would be your next bid if you held Peter's hand? Two spades asking for kings? This would be the impulsive bid, but a little thought will prove it to be incorrect. There are two good reasons:

1. If, as was the case, I had no kings, I would be forced to bid two notrump. I would then have the doubtful privilege of playing three notrump with the strong hand exposed and the lead coming through it!

2. Asking for kings would have left Peter in control, without any clear picture of my hand. It was better to jump to three notrump, describing his hand accurately and letting me take over.

I would have passed had he bid two notrump, showing 23 to 25 points. As it was, he had to be lucky to make the game.

Suppose I had held two kings. Would the fact that Peter had failed to ask for them compel me to pass? Far from it. I knew he had a very strong balanced hand and could use any high cards I held. With two kings I would have bid at least four notrump.

A long suit with a little high-card strength would also have been useful. A hand like:

♠ J x   ♡ K xx   ◊ Q 10 xxx   ♣ xxx

would probably have been ample for a slam.

A two diamond opening is more often based on distributional values than on a balanced hand. In the same tournament, Peter held this hand:

LEVENTRITT	SCHENKEN
♠ A Q	♠ xxx
♡ A K J 10 xxxx	♡ x
◊ A x	◊ K J xxx
♣ x	♣ A xxx
2 ◊ (aces?)	3 ♣ (club ace)
3 ◊ (kings?)	4 ◊ (diamond king)
4 ♡ (queens?)	4 ♠ (no queens)
6 ♡ (signoff)	Pass

When Peter bid four hearts he was, by coincidence, bidding his long suit, but as it was the cheapest bid, it was still conventional.

Six hearts was a fine contract but, alas, could not be made. A club was opened. The heart and diamond queens failed to drop, and the spade finesse lost. However, knowing that I held two sure tricks for him, only a coward would stop short of slam.

One more example, showing how vital cards were located for a grand slam at rubber bridge. Richard L. Frey was my partner.

SCHENKEN	FREY
♠ A K Q J xxx	♠ x
♡ ——	♡ J xxx
◊ A xxx	◊ K Q xx
♣ A K	♣ J xxx
2 ◊ (aces?)	2 ♡ (none)
2 ♠ (kings?)	3 ◊ (diamond king)
3 ♡ (queens?)	4 ◊ (diamond queen)
7 ♠	Pass

With twelve sure tricks in sight, I felt grand slam was a good gamble. When diamonds broke I made the hand easily, but I would also have made it if the club queen could be ruffed out, or if the same player had the long clubs and diamonds. How easy it was to reach this grand slam on only 28 high-card points!

In his fine book *According to Silodor & Tierney,* Sidney Silodor sets forth an inviolable rule for opening a game-forcing natural two bid. He requires at least four honor tricks, regardless of how many playing tricks the hand may have. He cites these hands which he would open *one* spade:

♠ A K Q J 9 6 2   ♡ ———   ◇ K Q J 10   ♣ 6 3

♠ K Q J 10 9 8   ♡ A K Q J 10   ◇ 3   ♣ 5

Here is Silodor's comment on these hands:

"With just three losers it will go against the grain of many not to open a two bid. However, the required four honor tricks are not present. There is less chance of missing game than there is that the partnership might arrive at an unmakable slam contract."

Using natural two bids and responses, Silodor is probably right in his contention. The fact remains that these two examples are ideally suited to the Schenken two diamond bid. With opener controlling the final contract, responder cannot take the level too high.

When the Opponents Interfere

What happens when the opponents enter the bidding (as they will now and then)? Suppose a non-jump overcall is made. As the primary aim is to get to game or slam, a double by responder is not for penalties—it simply shows the ace of that suit. Other responses are the same as if the opponent had passed, although the level is higher.

What if an opponent makes a jump overcall of three hearts or spades? Again a double shows the ace. A higher bid shows an ace of that suit, but here responder should have some extra values since this is a high level to start showing aces.

Summary

Two diamonds shows a balanced hand with 23 or more points, or a freakish game-going hand with slam possibilities. Opener's long suit should be solid or semi-solid.

With no aces, responder bids two hearts. With one ace he bids it, except that two notrump shows the heart ace. With two aces, responder single-jumps in the suit of the higher ace; with three aces, he double-jumps. A diamond rebid by opener asks responder to specify a second ace.

Over two hearts, two notrump by opener shows 23 to 25 points, and may be passed; three notrump shows 26 or 27 points. A suit rebid by opener is a game force.

The cheapest rebid by opener asks responder to show kings in the same manner he showed aces. Over the response, a diamond bid by opener asks for the second king (if possible); the cheapest bid asks for queens.

PART III

♣

COMPETITIVE BIDDING

There are several main aspects to successful competitive bidding:

1. Opening suit bids of one, two, three, or even more frequently make it difficult for the opponents to reach their best contract.

2. The higher the bid the more difficult becomes the opponents' task, but any opening bid usually works to their disadvantage.

3. When your side opens the bidding it often paves the way for a profitable sacrifice bid. Conversely, when you pass originally, good sacrifice bids become difficult to foresee or too dangerous to attempt.

15: *The Weak Two Bid*

[WARNING: DANGEROUS IF USED IMPROPERLY]

The weak two bid has always been my favorite, possibly because I invented it, way back in the 1930s when I played on the Four Aces team. It came about for two reasons:

First: I was always dissatisfied with the game-forcing two bid. The requirements for its use were so high that days might go by without anyone getting one. Thus it lapsed into a state of disuse.

Furthermore, I disliked the artificial response of two notrump to show a bust. This was not because it was artificial, but because it was impractical. If the hand wound up at a notrump contract, the strong hand was exposed with the lead coming through it. In addition, the opponents could easily see the best defense. Results were often disastrous.

Second: Our team was the first to use a single-jump overcall as a preemptive bid. The hand usually consisted of a six-card suit with substantial playing strength, and at least one but not more than two defensive tricks. The "weak" jump overcall had two distinct assets:

1. It informed partner that you could take five or six tricks at your suit; that you did not need strong trump support and might therefore take a profitable sacrifice against an opposing game contract.

2. It deprived the opponents of a round of bidding. This had a

twofold advantage. They might be shut out, or they might stretch to an unsafe level.

The weak jump overcall was so effective that I have used it ever since. From it developed the idea for the weak two bid. Surely if the weak jump overcall could make things difficult for the opponents, an opening bid made at the two-level *before* they have had a chance to bid should act as even more of a hindrance.

Hence the weak two bid. As opening bids of two clubs and two diamonds are used for other purposes in the Schenken System, weak two bids are made only in the major suits.

While nearly all experts and at least 75 per cent of tournament players have adopted these bids, I consider them optional, for these reasons:

1. They are not indispensable, as you can bid quite accurately without them, using the methods advocated in Part I.

2. To most players an opening suit bid of two means "forcing to game." To use this bid as "weak" and "non-forcing" might not appeal to you.

3. While I believe these bids are very effective, they will work only when properly understood. When used on a hand which is too strong, or even more importantly, too weak, they can boomerang and lose points instead of gaining them.

Many tournament and rubber bridge players fall so in love with the word "weak" that they use the weak two bid as a toy, usually with disastrous results. Make no mistake, I am proud of this bid, but wanted to voice my misgivings. Here are *my* requirements for the weak two bid:

1. A point count of 8 to 12 including at least 1½ and usually not more than two defensive tricks (except under certain conditions which I will explain later).

2. A six-card suit with at least two honors, Q-J or better, or a five-card suit with at least three honors, K-Q-10 or better.

3. At least five playing tricks, often six or more, especially when vulnerable.

♠ Q J 10 9 xx   ♡ x   ◇ A J 10 x   ♣ xx   8 pts.

Bid two spades. This hand has at least six playing tricks.

♠ A K Q xxx   ♡ xx   ◇ xxx   ♣ xx   9 pts.

Bid two spades—5½ playing tricks.

♠ xx   ♡ A Q J xx   ◇ Q J 10 xx   ♣ x   10 pts.

Bid two hearts. This hand will produce at least seven tricks if
partner fits either suit.

♠ x   ♡ K J 10 xxx   ◇ xx   ♣ A xxx   8 pts.

Bid two hearts. About five-plus playing tricks.

Each of the above examples will win more tricks than a typical
opening one spade bid, such as:

♠ K Q xxx   ♡ xx   ◇ K xx   ♣ A xx   12 pts.

which has about four-plus tricks. However, there are more high
cards here to combine with partner's hand.

♠ A 9 xxxx   ♡ xx   ◇ A xx   ♣ xx   8 pts.

Pass. The spade suit is too weak.

♠ K 10 9 xx   ♡ Q 10 x   ◇ A J 10 x   ♣ x   10 pts.

Pass, or if not vulnerable, bid *one* spade if you wish. This is the
wrong type of hand for a weak two bid. The spade suit is a weak-
ish five-carder. Another flaw is support for the other major, which
your partner should not expect. Remember, a weak two bid takes
bidding room away from partner as well as the opponents.

Third and Fourth Hand Weak Two Bids

When you are in third position, the only player you greatly fear
is seated at your left. Naturally you wish to force him to guess as
much as possible, hence you may open a little lighter or a little
stronger. Such hands as:

♠ K Q J 10 xx   ♡ xx   ◇ xxx   ♣ A Q   12 pts.

♠ xx   ♡ K J 10 9 xx   ◇ K xx   ♣ xx   7 pts.

may be opened with weak two bids, although the first has 2½ defensive tricks and 6½ playing tricks, while the second has only one-plus defensive tricks and 4½ playing tricks. These are the top and bottom limits for a third-hand weak two bid.

In fourth position you are free to pass out the deal, and should bid only if a profit appears likely.

♠ K x   ♡ K J 10 9 xx   ◇ xx   ♣ A J x   12 pts.

♠ K Q J 9 xx   ♡ xx   ◇ x   ♣ A J 10 x   11 pts.

♠ x   ♡ Q 10 9 xxx   ◇ A Q x   ♣ K J x   12 pts.

These are acceptable weak two bids in fourth position only. In all other positions, they should be opened with a one bid. You expect to make a part-score, and quite possibly a game if partner's cards fit.

The reason for bidding two rather than one is that if partner, by some unkind fate, holds the worst of the other three hands, the opponents—if not partially shut out—might "steal" the part-score, and once in a while, a game. On the other hand, if an opponent gets frisky, partner may be able to make a pleasing penalty double.

Two Bids with a Part-Score

Nearly all good players agree that when a part-score situation exists, it is best to get in the first blow by opening the bidding if possible. The weak two bid is ideally suited to this strategy.

I was North on this hand from a rubber bridge game. Both sides were vulnerable and the opponents had 40 on score:

NORTH
♠ 9 5
♡ K J 10 8 5 2
◇ A J 5
♣ 5 2

WEST   EAST
♠ A J 8 3   ♠ K Q 10 7 6 2
♡ 6 3   ♡ 9 4
◇ K 10 9 2   ◇ 6 4
♣ A 8 6   ♣ K Q 10

SOUTH
♠ 4
♡ A Q 7
◇ Q 8 7 3
♣ J 9 7 4 3

The bidding was:

NORTH	EAST	SOUTH	WEST
2 ♡	2 ♠	3 ♡	3 ♠
Pass	Pass	4 ♡	4 ♠
Pass	Pass	Pass	

We were lucky enough to win two tricks in both hearts and diamonds, for a one-trick set.

What would have happened if I had passed originally? East, also playing weak two bids, would have opened two spades. Partner had no sign of a bid, and West would have made things more difficult by raising to three spades.

Now I might have been brazen enough to bid four hearts, but I doubt it. It was far too risky. If partner's hand did not fit, I might easily have been set 1100 points.

The lesson is clear: the weak two heart bid provided the one chance to enter the fray without much risk.

The best tactics depend somewhat on your position at the table. Suppose for example you have 40 on score, both sides are vulnerable, and you are lucky enough to pick up this hand:

♠ A K Q xx   ♡ A Q 10   ◊ K J 10   ♣ xx

Playing the Schenken System you have a very sound one club opening, and in first or second position should surely make that bid.

But suppose you are third or fourth hand. How about opening with a "weak" two bid? You have hardly any chance for a slam, and two spades is enough for rubber. True, you are deceiving your partner, but surely he will forgive you if an opponent bids three in a red suit and you double and set him 800 or more points.

Sacrifice Bids

The weak two bid announces a good suit, and I cannot over-emphasize the importance of this. Partner may raise with what would be considered inadequate trump support for an opening one bid.

This paved the way for a profitable sacrifice in the following hand, where I was a spectator:

```
                    NORTH
                    ♠ J 6
                    ♡ 6 5
                    ◊ A Q 9 4 2
                    ♣ K 8 5 4
      WEST                                EAST
      ♠ A 8                               ♠ 10 5 3
      ♡ A K Q 7 4                         ♡ J 10 8 3
      ◊ 5 3                               ◊ 10 8
      ♣ Q J 10 6                          ♣ A 9 3 2
                    SOUTH
                    ♠ K Q 9 7 4 2
                    ♡ 9 2
                    ◊ K J 7 6
                    ♣ 7
```

Both sides were vulnerable; South dealer.

SOUTH	WEST	NORTH	EAST
2 ♠	3 ♡	3 ♠	4 ♡
4 ♠	Double	Pass	Pass
Pass			

South lost two hearts, a spade, and a club. The 200-point penalty was a bargain compared to the opponents' vulnerable game.

The feature of the bidding was North's raise to three spades on J-x. Suppose South had passed originally. West would bid one heart, pass by North, and two hearts by East. South would over-call with two spades, but West would jump to four hearts.

It would then be up to North. With fairly good defense and only two spades, I doubt if he would have ventured four spades. In turn, four spades by South would be a wild gamble that I could not condone.

Penalty Doubles

In view of the sparseness of high-card strength it would appear that not many sizable penalty doubles could be obtained after a weak two opening.

But strangely enough, many large sets accrue, for the two bid excites many opponents who refuse to be shut out even on very dubious holdings. Some of these gallant overcallers will come in at the three level, and if not immediately doubled, will bid up to four or five.

In the following hand, East was the dealer, with neither side vulnerable.

NORTH
♠ K 8 4
♡ 7 2
◇ K 7
♣ A J 10 9 6 3

WEST
♠ Q 5
♡ K J 9 6
◇ 10 8 3 2
♣ K 8 4

EAST
♠ A J 10 7 6 2
♡ 4
◇ Q J 6 4
♣ Q 5

SOUTH
♠ 9 3
♡ A Q 10 8 5 3
◇ A 9 5
♣ 7 2

EAST	SOUTH	WEST	NORTH
2 ♠	3 ♡	Pass	4 ♣
Pass	4 ♡	Double	Pass
Pass	Pass		

According to my definition of weak two bids, East's bid of two spades was just about perfect. He had a reasonable amount of defensive strength and, as declarer, would win about six tricks with any reasonable distribution of the cards.

South's overcall was decidedly shaky but West let it go by, as a double was slightly risky.

Under normal circumstances, North's four club bid was not bad, but he reckoned without his doughty partner. South remembered that three hearts had not been doubled, and therefore only a coward would fail to rebid such a fine six-card suit.

South lost two spade tricks, three heart tricks, and a club trick, for a 500-point gift penalty. Was he unlucky? Not at all. If North did not have heart support, as his four club takeout indicated, the trumps were bound to be bunched in West's hand.

The exciting effect of the weak two bid deserves credit for the gain to East-West. If East had passed his hand, it is most unlikely that his opponents would have gotten so high.

Responses to the Weak Two Bid

Most experts agree with the principles of the Schenken weak two bid, although some shade the requirements to an appalling degree. However, in theory at least, there is general agreement on what constitutes a proper bid.

But when it comes to responses, there are two distinct schools:

1. *"Every response is forcing except a raise."* This may work out well whenever responder has a very good hand with slam possibilities. It also may provide an opportunity for an occasional psychic response that may mislead weak opponents.

As against these virtues, there are a number of defects. The partnership must get to at least the three-level, but the quality of the opening bid may remain a mystery to responder. Thus it will be difficult for him to know when to stop.

For many years I also played all responses as forcing, but I have become convinced that better results can be obtained by playing:

2. *Two notrump as the only forcing response.* The two notrump response always shows at least the equivalent of an opening bid, although not necessarily a notrump-type hand. This is in itself an asset, as the opponents cannot safely enter the auction.

This response has two other distinct virtues:

1. In rebidding, opener can more clearly define his hand. With a minimum he simply rebids his suit. Or he can show another suit. Or he can even bid three notrump with a solid suit, or a good suit with a reentry.

2. Far more important, it gives responder the chance to play the hand at two or three of another suit. In addition, the quality of responder's hand remains unknown to the opponents.

Opener is allowed to pass any suit takeout. This gives him a little more leeway in his weak two bids. It is especially useful for those players who are apt to shade them.

When Peter Leventritt and I played against the Italian team in 1961 at Buenos Aires, we gained a large swing on the following hand, deal 84:

NORTH
♠ K Q 10 5 4 3
♡ A 10 9
◊ J
♣ 9 8 2

WEST
♠ 9 8 7
♡ 8 5
◊ K Q 3
♣ A K J 10 4

EAST
♠ A 6 2
♡ Q J 4
◊ A 10
♣ Q 7 6 5 3

SOUTH
♠ J
♡ K 7 6 3 2
◊ 9 8 7 6 5 4 2
♣ ———

NORTH	EAST	SOUTH	WEST
(Leventritt)	(Forquet)	(Schenken)	(Garrozzo)
2 ♠	Pass	3 ◊	Pass
Pass	Pass		

We bid and made three diamonds, scoring 60 points plus 50 for the part-score. U.S.A.: +110 points.

At the other table:

NORTH	EAST	SOUTH	WEST
(D'Alelio)	(Silodor)	(Chiaradia)	(Kay)
2 ♠	Pass	Pass	3 ♣
Pass	3 ♠	Pass	3 NT
Pass	Pass	Pass	

Kay made three notrump. U.S.A.: +600 points. Net plus: 710 points.

This hand alone is a convincing argument in favor of using two notrump as the only forcing response to a weak two bid. The difference in responding to the opening weak two bid, which was bid at both tables, was directly responsible for our fine result on this hand.

The Italians play all responses as forcing. Therefore Chiaradia, who held the same hand as I, did not dare to respond to his partner's weak two bid, as this would force opener to rebid. After the pass, Kay and Silodor had no difficulty in arriving at three notrump.

We were under no such restrictions. In fact, it was obvious to me that if I passed, my opponent would surely enter the auction. At the same time, my bid was not dangerous. It was simply a denial of Leventritt's spade suit, and he was almost duty-bound to pass.

Some other examples, assuming that partner has opened with two hearts:

♠ K x   ♥ Q x   ♦ A 10 xxx   ♣ A 10 xx

Respond two notrump, then pass a rebid of three hearts.

♠ xx   ♥ J xxx   ♦ A J xxx   ♣ Q x

Not vulnerable, bid four hearts as a shutout bid; vulnerable, bid three hearts.

♠ A K J xxx   ♥ x   ♦ xxx   ♣ xxx

Respond two spades. This is a denial of partner's suit. He should pass unless his suit is solid or he can raise spades.

♠ A K J xxx   ♥ x   ♦ A xx   ♣ A xx

Respond two notrump. Over a three heart rebid, bid three spades, a forcing bid.

♠ A K Q J xx   ♥ xx   ♦ Q 10 x   ♣ xx

Jump to three spades. This response shows a very good spade suit. While encouraging, it is not forcing.

♠ xx   ♡ K x   ◇ A 10 xxx   ♣ 10 xxx

If not vulnerable, bid three hearts. This is a further attempt to make life difficult for the opponents, who undoubtedly hold the better hands. Partner must pass this raise. If you were interested in game, you would first bid two notrump.

16: *The Weak Jump Overcall*

This bid was mentioned briefly in the last chapter as an introduction to the weak two bid. Having described the latter in detail, I believe the former deserves further discussion.

Before proceeding, I would like to place this bid also in the optional category. At the same time I would like to assert that the weak jump overcall is a most effective weapon (always with a penetrating eye fixed on the vulnerability conditions). While it can be played independently of the weak two bid, the two different bids are of the same family. If you like to play one, you will probably enjoy playing both.

The weak jump overcall is much simpler than the weak two bid. It is nothing more than an overcall one level higher than necessary.

When an opponent opens with one of a suit and you jump-overcall, you are depriving your left-hand opponent of at least one full bidding level. This often makes matters difficult for him. He may have a fair hand, but the level may be too high for him to bid, especially as his partner is now forced to rebid. Or, refusing to be shut out, he may stretch a doubtful hand with unfortunate results.

The weak two bid usually shows 1½ to 2 defensive tricks. The weak jump overcall may have only one. I have found it of the utmost importance to have this one trick, and rarely would I bid without it.

The playing strength required depends on the level at which

you bid, the vulnerability, and the strength of your suit. Put in a practical-if-mercenary way, the decision whether or not to make a jump overcall rests on the answers to these two questions: How much can I gain? How much can I lose? For example, your right-hand opponent opens one diamond. You are not vulnerable, and hold:

♠ K Q J xxx   ♡ xx   ◇ J xx   ♣ Q x

♠ x   ♡ A J 10 xxx   ◇ xx   ♣ J xxx

♠ xx   ♡ xx   ◇ K x   ♣ A Q J xxxx

With the first two hands I would bid respectively two spades and two hearts. I might be set 500 points, but if so, I have lost only slightly more than the value of a non-vulnerable game. But if vulnerable, a three-trick set would amount to 800 points, and this would be too much to lose. I would simply pass.

What about the third hand? Here I am likely to win seven tricks, and would therefore not be risking too much, even if vulnerable. The hand qualifies for a sound overcall of two clubs, but because of the weakness in the major suits, I vote for three clubs as a more effective bid.

This brings up several points worth mentioning. It should be obvious that more playing strength is needed to jump to the three-level. When your suit is a minor, particularly clubs, you should not risk too much. If you do, you give your opponents the choice of doubling or outbidding you at the same level. On the other hand, when you have a ranking suit, particularly spades, you can risk more. To buy the contract in a suit, the opponents must always bid one level higher. Your side can outbid them at the same level, and you may be able to sacrifice profitably at four spades when the opponents can make four hearts.

Some players make this distinction: not vulnerable, their jump overcalls are weak; vulnerable, they are strong. At the same time, they take no cognizance of whether the opponents are vulnerable or not. This arbitrary stand ignores the vital matter I mentioned before, namely, what can you lose and what can you gain?

Of course, if the opponents are not vulnerable, I do not risk more than 500 points. With both sides vulnerable, I would also like to hold my potential loss to this amount, but by risking a maximum of 800 points, I might wind up with a profit by pushing them beyond their depth, or occasionally shutting them out of the bidding.

One other thing I have noticed: When the opponents are vulnerable and we are not, they rarely stop to double at the first opportunity. Rather, they will go ahead and bid their game to make the maximum score. Therefore, under these conditions, I might jump a little lighter than normally.

A few more examples. Let's assume a vulnerable opponent opens the bidding with one heart. You are next and hold:

♠ K xxxxx   ♡ xx   ◇ K J 9   ♣ xx

With such a weak suit my preference is to pass. Change the hand to:

♠ K J 9 xxx   ♡ xx   ◇ K xx   ♣ xx

and I would risk two spades. If vulnerable, I would pass.

♠ A Q J xxx   ♡ x   ◇ A xx   ♣ K xx

Only a poor player would bid two spades with this strong hand. The only correct bid is to double, and then bid spades after partner has responded. This procedure shows a good hand with at least five good spades.

♠ K J 10 9 8 7 6   ♡ x   ◇ xx   ♣ Q J 10

Bid three spades! You have six sure playing tricks, but practically no defensive strength. When trying to make things difficult for the opponents, always preempt to the fullest extent possible with reasonable safety.

♠ A Q J 9 xx   ♡ K x   ◇ xx   ♣ xxx

♠ K Q J 10 xx   ♡ xx   ◇ A xx   ♣ xx

Both these hands are sound one spade overcalls. Nevertheless, I prefer to bid two spades on each of them. What about a jump to three spades? Rather than try to shut the opponents out of the bidding, I prefer to encourage them to bid. They might get to three notrump, which we would almost surely set. Or they might double prematurely, thereby presenting us with a game.

Summary

The jump overcall, like the weak two bid, is semi-preemptive in character. While it does not have the scope of the weak two bid, it does keep the opponents guessing. This is particularly so if you sometimes use it with hands like the last two discussed, which would be sound weak two bids.

17: *Who's Vulnerable?—or, When to Take Risks*

In most books on bridge the opponents seldom, if ever, bid. One book on point-count bidding, which I once waded through, started off with a fifty-page chapter. I was duly advised of the number of points needed for every conceivable bid, response, rebid, etc.

Even if I had the patience, I could not have memorized all these statistics. And while the two partners were point-counting back and forth, what were the opponents doing? Silent as the night!

Alas, it has never been my lot to encounter this bidding Utopia. Bridge, as I know it, is not played like this, whether it be rubber bridge or tournament play. The nasty fellows I play against are always opening, preempting, overcalling, jump-overcalling, and even psyching. Also they double. They double for takeout, and if I get too frisky, they double for penalties.

In other words, they are alive, not burying their heads in the sand while I bid without opposition. And this is why contract bridge is such an interesting game.

In previous chapters I have frequently mentioned the course of action I deem advisable in competitive bidding. The matter of vulnerability is all-important. What might be a perfectly proper bid (or at least a good gamble) in one set of circumstances would be sheer folly in another. As an illustration, suppose you are *third* hand and hold:

♠ xxx ♡ A Q J 9 x ◇ Q xx ♣ xx

1. If the opponents are vulnerable and you are not, a bid of one heart is perfectly proper. You do not expect to play the hand, but are indicating the best lead. You are prepared to pass any bid partner makes. Therefore you have much more to gain than you have to lose. Even without the outside queen I would recommend this bid in third position.

2. With neither side vulnerable, to bid is a good gamble.

3. With both sides vulnerable, to bid is a fair gamble. You have just about as much to gain as to lose.

4. If you are vulnerable and the opponents are not, to bid is a very poor gamble. For one thing your partner will expect more. For another, the player at your left, who probably has a good hand, may pass to trap you. When you now pass your partner's response, the trapper will now almost surely double. The result may well be that your side goes down 500 to 800 points. Too much to lose!

The moral is: Never stick your neck out when the vulnerability is unfavorable. If you do, the ax will probably descend.

All of the foregoing is based on the assumption that you have an intelligent partner. By this I mean a partner who will realize that a third-hand bid may be for lead-directing purposes, or simply in the hope of obtaining a part-score.

But if he is the type who believes in only "honest" bidding, do not open such a hand under any circumstances. If you do, your partner may jump to game in your suit, jump to two or three notrump, or double the opponents unsuccessfully.

The danger of these disasters is very great in most other systems. In fact, the word "leeway"—in this case making allowances for possible light opening bids in third position—is largely missing in American bidding.

To Bid or Not to Bid Game

One of the problems that arises frequently is whether to stop at a part-score or to bid game on a doubtful hand. Here the strategy of a loser is the opposite of that of a winner. You may hear the former say, after bidding game and being set one or two tricks, perhaps doubled, "Well, partner, I wasn't vulnerable, so I thought I would take a chance. It didn't cost much." This is completely wrong. It would have been better to push vulnerable than not vulnerable!

Let's assume you go down 50 points at four spades. What did it cost? Ninety for three spades, plus the 50 you lost, is 140. Furthermore, the unseen value of a part-score is at least 100 points, at times much more. When one side wins a larger rubber, it is often because the other side was feverishly defending against a part-score.

The *minimum* loss is therefore $100 + 90 + 50 = 240$ points. Now suppose you stop at three spades and make four. What have you lost? The game you missed is worth on the average 300 points, for a total of 420 points. But you gained 120 points plus 100 for the part-score, or 220 points. Your net loss is 200 points.

From this arithmetic it should be obvious that when you are not vulnerable, you should have *at least* an even chance for game. But when you are vulnerable a game is worth much more, while the loss if you go down is only slightly greater. So you should bid game on about a 40 per cent chance (if you are reasonably certain you will not be set more than one trick). This discussion should be worth a great many points to those "non-vulnerable gamblers."

You cannot always accurately estimate your chances for making game. Sometimes the hands will fit so well that every high card and distributional value can be utilized. At other times some high cards or distributional values turn out to be useless. In general, you should assume that the combined hands fit reasonably well. Some examples:

♠ A Q 10 x x   ♡ A J x   ◇ x x   ♣ J 10 x

If partner raises your one spade bid to two (constructive in the Schenken System), you should pass. If he jump-raises to three (invitational but not forcing), you should pass if not vulnerable, but bid game if vulnerable.

♠ A Q 10 xx ♡ A J x ◇ x ♣ J 10 xx

Pass a raise to two spades if not vulnerable, but bid three if vulnerable. Carry a jump raise to game on any vulnerability.

♠ A Q 10 xx ♡ A J x ◇ x ♣ Q 10 xx

Bid three over a single raise if not vulnerable, but jump to game if vulnerable. The fit will determine the result—but vulnerable you have more to gain.

Part-Score Bidding

I have found that when either we or our opponents have a part-score it pays to open all borderline hands. When we have the part-score, we need only another part-score for game. When the opponents have the part-score, it is far less dangerous to open the bidding than to come in later after an opponent has opened.

These statements are dependent on your partner (as is so much in bridge). If he is conservative, or clever enough to allow some leeway, I pursue the course outlined above. But if he is an optimist, a gallant defender, or just tenacious, I have to stick with sound book bids. They will not hinder the opponents as much, but will at any rate keep *us* out of serious trouble.

As always, the vulnerability is often the deciding factor.

With favorable vulnerability, I believe in competing vigorously. If I overbid two or three tricks and am doubled, I still have a chance for the rubber. In the process I may push the opponents beyond their depth.

With equal vulnerability, I try not to be set more than 500 points. Once in a great while I may suffer a larger set; far more often I will maneuver the opponents into an unmakable contract.

When I have a part-score, I try to avoid bidding a weak suit—particularly if my bid completes the part-score. For example:

♠ A Q xx   ♡ K Q xx   ◇ xx   ♣ A xx

With 60 or less on score I would open this hand one spade and, if given the chance, bid hearts later. However, with 70 or more on score, one spade might be passed, and prove to be the only contract I cannot make. So I would open a slightly shaded one notrump.

Responder also should not bid a shaky suit if his bid is enough for game. However, he may respond with less in high cards than is usual in the Schenken System.

Assume you have 60 on score, and partner opens one heart. You hold:

♠ 10 xx   ♡ xx   ◇ A 10 xxx   ♣ A K x

Respond one notrump. (With no score, bid two diamonds.)

♠ xx   ♡ xx   ◇ K Q 10 xxx   ♣ xxx

Respond two diamonds. (With no score, pass.)

♠ Q J xx   ♡ xx   ◇ A J xx   ♣ Q xx

Respond one spade—forcing. But with 70 or more on score, bid one notrump.

♠ Q J xx   ♡ x   ◇ A J xx   ♣ A Q xx

Respond one notrump. This completes your part-score, and is a perfect trap bid. If an opponent raises his head, you can chop it off.

If partner bids beyond game in your suit, you are encouraged to continue, but should pass with little extra. However, a jump shift is forcing. Partner may have a slam hand, but be in doubt as to where to play it.

Overcalls and Takeout Doubles

When an opponent has a part-score and opens the bidding, you should compete with doubtful values, though you might not if he had no score. You should also stretch to compete if *you* have the part-score, for you may be able to romp off with the game.

Thus some risks should be taken, bearing in mind as always the vulnerability and your partner. Assume the opponents have 60 on score, and you hold:

♠ xx   ♡ A Q 10 9 xx   ◇ xxx   ♣ xx

Opponent opens one spade. With favorable or equal vulnerability, bid two hearts. If you are vulnerable and the opponents not, the risk is too great—pass.

♠ K J 9 xx   ♡ K xx   ◇ xxx   ♣ xx

Opponent opens one heart. This is a reasonable overcall of one spade, not vulnerable.

♠ x   ♡ xxxx   ◇ A J 10 xx   ♣ A J x

Opponent opens one spade. Double for takeout. This gives partner a choice of three suits, and is far better than a two diamond overcall, even though you have only 10 points in high cards.

Summary

The vulnerability should be taken into account at all times. Not vulnerable, bid for game only with at least a 50 per cent chance. Vulnerable, bid for game with at least a 40 per cent chance.

In all competitive auctions, where both sides are bidding, watch the vulnerability particularly carefully. Compete vigorously with equal or favorable vulnerability. Be very wary when you are vulnerable and they are not.

In part-score situations, open all borderline hands, and shade your overcalls and takeout doubles.

When competing, ask partner to allow you some leeway. He should not take your bids too literally, bid too strongly, or double for penalties without very sound reasons—usually, good trumps. Give your partner as much leeway as you want for yourself.

PART IV

♣

THE SYSTEMS
COMPARED

18: *Who's Afraid of the Big Bad Partner?*

After my many years' experience in playing Standard American with players whose ability varied from palooka to expert, I have reached this conclusion: American experts are afraid of their partners! The more expert they are, the more they fear their partner's bidding.

This fact runs right through the entire system of bids and responses.

Consider first the game-forcing two bid. Goren reduced it to this formula: Open with a game-forcing two bid if you hold at least:

25 points and a five-card suit, or
23 points and a six-card suit, or
21 points and a seven-card suit

Silodor has stated that it is an inviolable rule of his never to open with a game-forcing bid unless he holds at least four honor tricks, no matter how many playing tricks his hand contains.

These never-to-be-broken rules eliminate from consideration hands such as:

♠ K Q J 10 xxx ♡ A K Q J ◇ x ♣ x

♠ ——— ♡ A K Q J xxx ◇ A Q J x ♣ xx

Both are practically sure game hands, yet in Standard American they are opened with a one bid. No matter how weak the opposite hand is, a game may be missed.

Why are experts afraid to open with a two bid on such hands? Only one answer—fear of partner. He may have some high cards, particularly kings and queens that do not fit opener's hand, and may drive to an unmakable slam.

Partner is unrestricted in his responses. If, for example, he holds a solid minor suit, nothing will keep him out of slam after his partner has opened with a two bid!

Our European friends have no such inhibitions about game-forcing bids, because their partners are kept on a leash. When the Schenken game-forcing two diamond bid is used on strong distributional hands such as above, partners are likewise restrained. They simply are not allowed to take control.

Let's take up next the matter of responding to an opening suit bid of one. Many experts maintain they never pass. Why? They are afraid to. For one thing, they are afraid to reveal utter weakness by passing. Secondly—and in direct contradiction to the first reason—they are afraid of missing a game.

Playing the Schenken System, you need not fear either of these calamities. Unless you have at least 9 or 10 points, or strong distributional support for partner's suit, you know that game is most improbable. So you can pass your partner's opening bid with as much as 7 or 8 points. This represents substantial defensive strength, hence the opponents would be foolish to consider you out of the picture. If, in fact, they reopen the bidding, you may be able to double them.

Let's pursue the matter of responding. In Standard American, while the bidding may be kept open with one of a suit or one no-trump on as little as 3, 4, or 5 points, in order to make a positive response (a two-over-one bid), responder needs at least 10 points. Thus, with a hand such as:

♠ xx   ♡ A Q J 9 xx   ◇ xxx   ♣ xx

the standard response to one spade is one notrump, which opener may pass. Obviously, this is likely to be an unsatisfactory contract.

Here once again, responder is afraid to bid two hearts for fear of what partner will do.

In some systems, the opening bidder always bids again over a one notrump response by an unpassed hand. Here, at least, a poor one notrump contract is avoided. On the second round of bidding responder can show his heart suit. But how can the opening bidder know that the suit contains five almost sure tricks?

I hasten to assure you that, playing the Schenken System, you would show your fine heart suit immediately. The two heart bid is forcing for one round only, and does not guarantee a further bid.

Two recent hands come to mind which further illustrate fear of partner. In the first hand I played the role of frustrated dummy.

PARTNER	SCHENKEN
♠ A Q 10 xxx	♠ xxx
♡ A K	♡ J 9 x
◇ xx	◇ A K 10 9 x
♣ A 10 x	♣ K x

The bidding was:

PARTNER	SCHENKEN
1 ♠	2 ◇
2 NT!	3 NT
Pass	

In explaining the bidding I would like to state that although my partner is considered to be one of the finest players in the country, he dislikes jump bids. To what extent I did not realize until after this hand.

True, I might have bid three spades over two notrump, but with a balanced hand, something in every suit, and only three small spades, three notrump seemed to be the easiest way to game. I never dreamed that a spade slam was almost cold!

Why didn't my partner, with his magnificent hand, jump to

three spades on the second round? Was he afraid of what I might do? Possibly, but more likely it was simply his "minimum forcing" style of bidding.

Playing the Schenken System he would of course open with one club, and after my positive response of two diamonds, we would have no trouble in getting to six spades.

The second hand, even more incredible, involved two lady experts who are reputed to be ultra-scientific bidders.

OPENER	RESPONDER
♠ Q xx	♠ A xx
♡ A K 10	♡ xx
◇ A	◇ K Q J xx
♣ K Q xxxx	♣ A 10 x

Their bidding:

OPENER	RESPONDER
1 ♣	1 ◇
1 ♡ !	3 ◇
3 ♠ !	3 NT
Pass!	

To the layman, opener's bidding may be difficult to fathom, and indeed, if I had not seen similar bidding many times (but seldom as bizarre as this), it would also be incomprehensible to me. I'll do my best to explain it.

The opening bid and response were normal expert practice, although some "amateurs" might use the game-forcing response of two diamonds. After the one diamond response, opener was faced with a dilemma. Two clubs was too weak, and three clubs or two notrump was too strong, she thought, for fear of what partner might do. Hence the compromise, one heart!

Responder quite correctly jumped to three diamonds. Opener was once again in a predicament. So far she had made only minimum bids, and yet she had a fine hand. How best to show it? By a sort of delayed "reverse" bid of three spades.

Alas, this bid only caused more confusion. Like many players nowadays, this lady never opens the bidding in a four-card major. Therefore her partner thought she had four cards in each major suit and only three or four clubs.

This ill-founded conclusion led responder to bid three notrump. She remarked later that if she had been confident her partner held a genuine club suit, she would have raised clubs. But she could not be sure, and therefore made the safe bid.

Opener might still have ventured four clubs or four notrump. But she did not, and thus while only game was bid, thirteen tricks were made.

With our artificial club opening, even two average players would have no trouble getting to at least a small slam.

19: *That First Round of Bidding*

The first round of bidding is the foundation on which later bidding must be built. One fact stands out clearly in a comparison of the Schenken System with Standard American: Even when the opening bid and the response are the same, in the Schenken System the strength shown is clearly defined. In Standard American the ranges are enormous, and each partner's hand is unknown to the other. Let me illustrate.

Schenken System	*Standard American*
An opening bid of one diamond, heart, or spade usually ranges from 12 to 16 high-card points.	An opening bid of one of a suit ranges from 12 to as many as 24 high-card points.
A one-over-one response ranges from 8 to 15 points. Game is possible, but slam is remote.	A one-over-one response ranges from 3 to 18 points. Any contract from part-score to grand slam is possible.
With fewer than 8 points, responder passes.	Responder seldom passes, for fear opener is loaded.
With slam interest and 15 points or more, responder makes a jump-shift response.	A jump-shift response requires 19 points or more, and is virtually forcing to slam.
A single raise is constructive—8 to 11 points. A double raise is invitational—12 or 13 points. No temporizing is necessary.	A single raise has a wider range—6 to 10 points. A jump raise is forcing to game—13 to 16 points. With 11 or 12 points, responder must invent a temporizing bid.

Schenken System

A one notrump response is constructive—9 to 11 points. Responder cannot have a long suit, for he can go to the two-level with as little as 7 points.

A two notrump response is invitational—12 or 13 points. A three notrump response is a signoff—14 or 15 points. No temporizing is necessary.

Standard American

A one notrump response has a wide range—5 to 10 points. Responder may have a long suit, but needs 10 points to go to the two-level.

A two notrump response is forcing to game—13 to 15 points. A three notrump response is a slam try—16 to 18 points. With 11 or 12 points, responder must invent a temporizing bid.

Next, consider how much information is exchanged in the first round of bidding in the Schenken System when the opening bid is *one club*. Responder knows immediately that opener has at least 17 points. If he responds one diamond, opener knows he has fewer than 9 points and 1½ honor tricks. If he makes any other response, both partners know that the combined hands total at least 26 points, and that game *at least* is assured.

Finally, I will summarize the other special opening bids of the Schenken System.

Two clubs: Rebiddable club suit, 11 to 15 points.

Two diamonds: Followed by two notrump—23 to 25 points.
Followed by three notrump—26 or 27 points.
Followed by a suit bid—game force on very strong suit. Opener is in command.

Two hearts or spades: (Optional) Weak two bid, good suit, 5 or 6 playing tricks.

Two notrump: (Optional) Solid minor suit, 17 to 20 points, about 7 playing tricks.

Three clubs: Solid club suit, 6 to 7 playing tricks.

Three notrump: (Optional) Solid minor suit, 17 to 22 points, about 8 playing tricks.

You will see that these many opening bids, together with the one-level opening bids, permit you to describe almost every type of hand, usually in one round or at most two rounds. Bidding is easier with the Schenken System.

20: *The Schenken System Summarized*

I. Hand Evaluation

High-card points: Ace = 4, King = 3, Queen = 2, Jack = 1.

As opening bidder, for a suit contract, add 1 point for the fourth card of any suit (Q-x-x-x, J-10-x-x, or better). Add an additional point for the fifth card of any suit, and 2 points for every card over five.

The point count undervalues a long solid suit or two very strong suits. Therefore, *count your playing tricks.*

As opening bidder or responder at notrump, use the high-card point evaluation, which is reasonably accurate.

When raising partner's suit, holding one or more trump honors, add 1 point. For each doubleton, add 1 point. For a singleton, add 3 points (2 points holding only three trumps). For a void, add 5 points (4 points holding only three trumps).

II. Opening Bid of One Club

Strong, artificial, forcing. At least 17 points including distribution:

1. Balanced notrump-type hand, 19–22 points.
2. Slightly unbalanced, 17 points or more.
3. Strong six-card suit or two-suit hand, 14 points or more.

Responses

One diamond: Negative, artificial. Fewer than 9 points and 1½ honor tricks. *Any other response is positive and forcing to game.*

One heart, one spade, two clubs, two diamonds: Natural positive responses—at least 9 points and 1½ honor tricks, five-card or longer (or very good four-card) suit.

A higher suit response: Solid or semi-solid suit.

One notrump: 9 to 11 points, balanced hand.

Two notrump: 12 or 13 points, balanced hand.

Over opponent's overcall (up to two spades): Double is "positive" (shows positive response), and requests takeout by opening club bidder.

Rebid by Opener After One Diamond Response

Non-jump suit rebid: May be passed.

Jump suit rebid: Forcing for one more round.

One notrump: 19 or 20 points, balanced hand; or a strong 18-point hand.

Two notrump: 21 or 22 points, balanced hand.

III. Opening Bid of One Notrump

16 to 18 points, balanced hand. Add 1 point for a good five-card suit.

Stayman Convention: In each of the following sequences, the cheapest club bid asks for a major suit:

1 NT	2 ♣		1 ♣	1 ◇		1 ♣	1 NT
			1 NT	2 ♣		2 ♣	
			1 ♣	1 ◇		1 ♣	2 NT
			2 NT	3 ♣		3 ♣	

IV. Opening Bid of One Diamond, One Heart, or One Spade

Limited range, usually 12 to 16 points.

Responses

Pass of opening bid: Game remote, 8 points or less.

Single raise: Constructive, 8 to 11 points.

Jump raise: Invitational (not forcing), 12 or 13 points.

Jump raise to game: Shutout, at least four trumps and 11–14 points (mostly distributional).

One notrump: Constructive, usually 9 to 11 points.

Two notrump: Invitational (not forcing), 12 or 13 points, balanced hand, stoppers in each unbid suit.

Three notrump: 14 or 15 points.

One-over-one: Constructive, at least 8 points.

Two-over-one: At least 10 points (may be as few as 7 points with good six-card suit).

Jump shift: Mild slam try, at least 15 points.

V. Opening Bid of Two Clubs

Six-card or longer (or good five-card) club suit, 11 to 15 points. Two notrump or jump-shift response is forcing.

VI. Opening Bid of Three Clubs

Solid club suit (usually six or seven cards), not more than 4 points outside the club suit.

VII. Opening Bid of Two Diamonds

Strong, artificial, forcing:

1. A notrump hand with 23 points or more.
2. Very strong solid or almost solid long suit—game force.

Responder *must* show aces (2 ♡ = none; 2 NT = heart ace; 2 ♠, 3 ♣, 3 ♢ = ace of that suit; single jump = that ace and an ace in a lower-ranking suit; double jump = three aces).

Rebids by Opener

Two notrump (over two hearts): 23 to 25 points, balanced

hand, the only rebid that may be passed below game if responder has nothing.

Three notrump: 26 or 27 points, balanced hand.

Cheapest rebid requests responder to show kings, then queens.

Cheapest rebid in diamonds asks responder to show second-highest ace.

VIII. Optional Bids

Two notrump opening: Solid minor suit, 7–8 playing tricks (17 to 20 points), at least Q-x in each side suit.

Three notrump opening: Solid minor suit, about 8–9 playing tricks (17 to 22 points), at least Q-x in each side suit.

Two heart or two spade opening: "Weak two bid"—good six-card suit, 8 to 12 points. Two notrump or jump-shift response is forcing.

Weak jump overcall: Similar to weak two bid.

IX. What to Tell Your Partner—A One-Minute Summary

1. My opening one club bid is artificial and shows a strong hand, 17 points or more, 14 points with a powerful one- or two-suit hand.

2. If you have less than 9 points, respond one diamond.

3. After your negative response of one diamond, if I rebid without jumping you may pass; if I jump in a suit you must respond again.

4. If you have 9 points or more, you make your natural response (with a diamond suit you must respond two diamonds). After your "positive" response, we may not pass short of game, since our combined hands must contain at least 26 points.

5. My opening one bids in the other suits are limited to at most 16 points. Don't bother to keep the bidding open on trash—you need 8 points or more.

6. If I open two clubs, it shows an ordinary one club bid with at least a good five-card club suit.

7. My opening three club bid shows a solid suit with 6 to 7 playing tricks.

8. My notrumps, takeout doubles, preempts, etc., are the same as yours.

PART V

APPENDIX

THE INTERNATIONAL CODE LAWS
OF CONTRACT BRIDGE 1963

The Scope of the Laws

The Laws are designed to define correct procedure and to provide an adequate remedy whenever a player accidentally, carelessly or inadvertently disturbs the proper course of the game, or gains an unintentional but nevertheless unfair advantage. An offending player should be ready to pay a prescribed penalty graciously.

The Laws are not designed to prevent dishonorable practices and there are no penalties to cover intentional violations. In the absence of penalty, moral obligations are strongest. Ostracism is the ultimate remedy for intentional offenses.

The object of the Proprieties is twofold: to familiarize players with the customs and etiquette of the game, generally accepted over a long period of years; and to enlighten those who might otherwise fail to appreciate when or how they are improperly conveying information to their partners—often a far more reprehensible offense than a violation of a law.

When these principles are appreciated, arguments are avoided and the pleasure which the game offers is materially enhanced.

Part 1   Definitions

Auction — 1. The process of determining the contract by means of successive calls. 2. The aggregate of calls made. 3. The period during which calls are made.

Bid — An undertaking to win at least a specified number of odd tricks in a specified denomination.

Call — Any bid, double, redouble, or pass.

Contract — The undertaking by declarer's side to win, at the denomination named, the number of odd tricks specified in the final bid, whether undoubled, doubled, or redoubled.

Convention — Any call or play which, by agreement or understanding between partners, serves to convey a meaning other than would be attributed to it by the opponents in the absence of an explanation.

Deal — 1. The distribution of the pack to form the hands of the four players. 2. The cards so distributed considered as a unit, including the auction and play thereof.

Declarer — The player who, for the side that makes the final bid, first bid the denomination named in that bid. He becomes declarer when the auction is closed.

Defective Trick — A trick that contains fewer or more than four legally played cards.

Defender — An opponent of declarer.

Denomination — The suit or no-trump specified in a bid.

Double — A call that increases the scoring values of odd tricks or undertricks at an opponent's bid.

Dummy — Declarer's partner. He becomes dummy when the auction is closed.

Follow Suit — To play a card of the suit that has been led.

Game — A unit in scoring denoting the accumulation of 100 or more trick points.

Hand — The cards originally dealt to a player or the remaining portion thereof.

Honor — Any Ace, King, Queen, Jack, or ten.

Irregularity — A deviation from the correct procedures set forth in the Laws and Proprieties.

Lead — The first card played to a trick.

Odd Trick — Each trick won by declarer's side in excess of six.

Opening Lead — The card led to the first trick.

Opponent — A player of the other side; a member of the partnership to which one is opposed.

Overtrick — Each trick won by declarer's side in excess of the contract.

Pack — The 52 playing cards with which the game of Contract Bridge is played.

Partial Designation — Incomplete specification by declarer of the rank or suit of a card to be played from dummy's hand (see Law 46).

Partner — The player with whom one plays as a side against the other two players.

Part Score — A unit in scoring denoting fulfillment of a contract of which the value is less than 100 trick points.

Pass — A call specifying that a player does not, at that turn, elect to bid, double, or redouble.

Penalty — An obligation or restriction imposed upon a side for violation of these Laws.

Penalty Card — A card that has been prematurely exposed by a defender and must be left face up on the table until legally played or permitted to be picked up.

Play — 1. The contribution of a card from one's hand to a trick, including the first card, which is the lead. 2. The aggregate of plays made. 3. The period during which the cards are played.

Premium Points — Any points earned other than trick points (see Law 75).

Rectification — Adjustment made to permit the auction or play to proceed as normally as possible after an irregularity has occurred.

Redeal — A second or subsequent deal by the same dealer to replace his first deal.

Redouble — A call that increases the scoring value of odd tricks or undertricks at a bid of one's own side that an opponent has doubled.

Revoke — The play of a card of another suit by a player who is able to follow suit.

Rotation — The order in which the right to deal, to call or to play progresses, which is clockwise.

Rubber — A unit in scoring denoting the winning of two games by a side.

Side — Two players who constitute a partnership against the other two players.

Slam — A contract to win twelve tricks, six odd tricks (called SMALL SLAM), or to win all thirteen tricks, seven odd tricks (called GRAND SLAM) ; also, the fulfillment of such a contract.

Specified Suit — Any suit that a player, in exacting a penalty, requires to be led or not to be led.

Suit — One of four groups of cards in the pack, each group comprising thirteen cards and having a characteristic symbol: spades (♠), hearts (♡), diamonds (◇), clubs (♣).

Trick — The unit by which the outcome of the contract is determined, regularly consisting of four cards, one contributed by each player in rotation, beginning with the lead.

Trick Points — Points earned by declarer's side by fulfilling the contract (see Law 75).

Trump — Each card of the suit, if any, named in the contract.

Turn — The correct time when a player may deal, call, or play.

Undertrick — Each trick by which declarer's side fails to fulfill the contract.

Vulnerability — The condition of being exposed to greater undertrick penalties and entitled to greater premiums, through having won one game toward the rubber (see Law 84).

Part 2   Preliminaries to the Rubber

1. *The players — The pack*

Contract Bridge is played by four players with a pack of 52 cards of identical back design and color, consisting of 13 cards in each of four suits. Two packs should be used, of which only one is in play at any time; and each pack should be clearly distinguishable from the other in back design or color.

2. *Rank of cards*

The cards of each suit rank in descending order: Ace, King, Queen, Jack, 10, 9, 8, 7, 6, 5, 4, 3, 2.

3. *The draw*

Before every rubber, each player draws a card from a pack shuffled and spread face down on the table. A card should not be exposed until all the players have drawn.

The two players who draw the highest cards play as partners against the two other players. When cards of the same rank are drawn, the rank of suits determines which is higher—spades (highest), hearts, diamonds, clubs.

The player with the highest card deals first and has the right to choose his seat and the pack with which he will deal. He may consult his partner but, having announced his decision, must abide by it. His partner sits opposite him. The opponents then occupy the two remaining seats as they wish and, having made their selection, must abide by it.

A player must draw again if he draws one of the four cards at either end of the pack, or a card adjoining one drawn by another player, or a card from the other pack; or if, in drawing, he exposes more than one card.

Part 3   The Deal

4. *The shuffle*

Before the cards are dealt they must be shuffled thoroughly, without exposure of the face of any card. The shuffle must be performed in full view of the players and to their satisfaction.

The pack to be used in each deal is prepared by the left-hand opponent of the player who will deal it. Preparation of the pack includes collecting the cards, shuffling them, and placing the shuffled pack face down at the left of the next dealer.

A pack properly prepared should not be disturbed until the dealer picks it up for his deal, at which time he is entitled to the final shuffle.

No player other than the dealer and the player designated to prepare the pack may shuffle.

5. *The cut*

The pack must always be cut immediately before it is dealt. The dealer presents the pack to his right-hand opponent, who lifts off a portion and places it on the table toward the dealer. Each portion must contain at least four cards. The dealer completes the cut by placing what was originally the bottom portion upon the other portion.

No player other than the dealer's right-hand opponent may cut the pack.

6. *New cut — New shuffle*

There must be a new cut if any player demands one before the first card is dealt. In this case the dealer's right-hand opponent cuts again.

There must be a new shuffle, followed by a cut:

A. If any player demands one before the dealer has picked up the pack for his deal. In this case the player designated to prepare the pack shuffles again.

B. If any player demands one after the dealer has picked up the pack but before the first card is dealt. In this case only the dealer shuffles.

C.   If a card is turned face up in shuffling. In this case the player who was shuffling shuffles again.

D.   If a card is turned face up in cutting. In this case only the dealer shuffles.

E.   If there is a redeal (see Law 10).

7.   *Change of pack*

The two packs are used alternately, unless there is a redeal.

A pack containing a card so damaged or marked that it may be identified from its back must be replaced if attention is drawn to the imperfection before the first card of the current deal is dealt.

A pack originally belonging to a side must be restored on demand of any player before the last card of the current deal has been dealt.

8.   *The deal*

The dealer distributes the cards face down, one at a time in rotation into four separate hands of thirteen cards each, the first card to the player on his left and the last card to himself. If he deals two cards simultaneously or consecutively to the same player, or fails to deal a card to a player, he may rectify the error, provided he does so immediately and to the satisfaction of the other players.

The dealer must not allow the face of any card to be seen while he is dealing. Until the deal is completed, no player but the dealer may touch any card except to correct or prevent an irregularity.

9.   *Rotation of the turn to deal*

The turn to deal passes in rotation, unless there is a redeal. If a player deals out of turn, and attention is not drawn to the error before the last card has been dealt, the deal stands as though it had been in turn, the player who dealt the cards is the dealer, and the player who has missed his turn to deal has no redress; and the rotation continues as though the deal had been in turn, unless a redeal is required under Law 10.

10.   *Redeal*

When there is a redeal, the current deal is canceled; the same dealer deals again, unless he was dealing out of turn; the same pack is used, unless it has been replaced as provided in Law 7; and the cards are shuffled and cut anew as provided in Laws 4 and 5.

There must be a redeal:

A.   If, before the last card has been dealt, it is discovered that

    i] a card has been turned face up in dealing or is face up in the pack or elsewhere;

    ii] the cards have not been dealt correctly;

    iii] a player is dealing out of turn or is dealing with a pack that was not shuffled or not cut, provided any player demands a redeal.

B.   If, before the first call has been made, it is discovered that a player has picked up another player's hand and has seen a card in it.

C.   If, before play has been completed, it is discovered that

    i] the pack did not conform in every respect to the requirements of Law I, including any case in which a missing card cannot be found after due search;

    ii] one player has picked up too many cards, another too few;

    iii] two or more players on opposing sides have allowed any cards from their hands to be mixed together, following a claim that a redeal is in order.

11. *Missing card*

When a player has too few cards and a redeal is not required by Law 10 C, the deal stands as correct, and:

A.   If he has played more than one card to a previous trick, Law 68 applies;

B.   If a missing card is found elsewhere than in a previous trick, that card is deemed to have belonged continuously to the deficient hand and must be restored to that hand; it may become a penalty card, as provided in Law 23 or 49, and failure to have played it may constitute a revoke.

12. *Surplus card*

When a player has too many cards and a redeal is not required by Law 10 C, the deal stands as correct, and:

A.   If the offender has omitted to play to a trick, Law 68 applies.

B.   If the offender has picked up a surplus card from a previous trick, or from dummy's hand, or from the other pack, or elsewhere, such surplus card must be restored to its proper place; and

    i] If the surplus card is in the offender's hand when it is discovered, there is no penalty.

ii] If the surplus card has been led or played, the offender must substitute for it a card from his hand that he can legally play to the trick and if possible a card of the same suit as the surplus card, and the offense is subject to the rectification and penalty provisions of Laws 62 to 65.

Part 4   General Laws Governing Irregularities

13. *Procedure following an irregularity*

When an irregularity has been committed, any player—except dummy as restricted by Law 43—may draw attention to it and give or obtain information as to the law applicable to it. The fact that a player draws attention to an irregularity committed by his side does not affect the rights of the opponents.

After attention has been drawn to an irregularity, no player should call or play until all questions in regard to rectification and to the assessment of a penalty have been determined. Premature correction of an irregularity on the part of the offender may subject him to a further penalty (see Law 26).

14. *Assessment of a penalty*

A penalty may not be imposed until the nature of the irregularity to be penalized has been determined and the applicable penalty has been clearly stated; but a penalty once paid, or any decision agreed and acted upon by the players, stands, even though at some later time it be adjudged incorrect.

With the exception of dummy, either member of the nonoffending side may impose a penalty, but without consulting his partner.

15. *Waiver or forfeiture of penalty*

The right to penalize an offense is forfeited if a member of the nonoffending side

A.   waives the penalty;

B.   consults with his partner as to the imposition of a penalty before a penalty has been imposed;

C.   calls (Law 34) or plays (Law 60) after an irregularity committed by the opponent at his right.

Rectification or validation proceeds as provided in the law applicable to the specific irregularity.

16. *Unauthorized information*

Any player except declarer may be subject to penalty if he conveys information to his partner other than by a legal call or play.

Information conveyed by an illegal call, play or exposure of a card is subject to the applicable law in Part V or VI.

If any player except declarer conveys information to his partner by means of a remark or an unmistakable gesture or mannerism that suggests a call,* lead, play, or plan of play; and if attention is drawn to the offense and the penalty is assessed forthwith, as provided in Laws 13 and 14:

A.   If the offense occurs before the auction closes, (penalty) either member of the nonoffending side may require both members of the offender's side to pass during the remainder of the auction; and if the offender becomes a defender, then when first it is the turn of the offender's partner to lead, including the opening lead, declarer may either

  i] require the offender's partner to lead a specified suit, or

  ii] prohibit the offender's partner from leading a specified suit; this prohibition continues for as long as the offender's partner retains the lead.

B.   If the offense occurs after the auction closes, (penalty) declarer or either defender, as the case may be, may prohibit the offender's partner from making:

  i] a lead improperly suggested; this prohibition applies to any one lead, including the opening lead, and continues for as long as the offender's partner retains the lead; or

  ii] a play improperly suggested; this prohibition may be applied to only one play.

The rights of the nonoffending side are not affected by an intervening call or play by the offending side. If the offender's partner has called after the offense, but before a member of the nonoffending side has subsequently called, his call may be canceled. If the offender's partner has led or played after the offense, and before a member of the nonoffending side has subsequently played, he may be required to withdraw his card and to substitute a card that does not conform to the improper suggestion, and a defender's card so withdrawn becomes a penalty card.

---

* After a deal has been completed, a player should not draw attention to the score, except to correct an error in recording. See Proprieties II G.

Part 5   The Auction

Correct Procedure

17.   *Duration of the auction*

The auction begins when the last card of a correct deal has been placed on the table. The dealer makes the first call, and thereafter each player calls in rotation. When three passes in rotation have followed any call, the auction is closed.

18.   *Bids*

Each bid must name a number of odd tricks, from one to seven, and a denomination. A bid supersedes the previous bid if it names either a greater number of odd tricks, or the same number of odd tricks in a higher denomination. A bid that fulfills these requirements is sufficient; one that does not, is insufficient. The denominations rank in descending order: no-trump, spades, hearts, diamonds, clubs.

19.   *Doubles and redoubles*

A player may double only the last preceding bid, and then only if it was made by an opponent and no call other than a pass has intervened.

A player may redouble only the last preceding double, and then only if it was made by an opponent and no call other than a pass has intervened.

A player should not, in doubling or redoubling, state the number of tricks or the denomination; but, if he states either or both incorrectly, he is deemed to have doubled or redoubled the bid as it was made.

All doubles and redoubles are superseded by a subsequent legal bid. If there is no subsequent bid, scoring values are increased as provided in Law 84.

20.   *Review of the auction*

A player who does not hear a call distinctly may forthwith require that it be repeated.

Before the auction closes, a player is entitled to have all previous calls restated when it is his turn to call, unless he is required by law to pass.

After the auction closes, declarer or either defender may require previous calls to be restated. A defender's right to such a review terminates when a member of his side has led or played to the first trick; declarer's right terminates when he has played to the first trick or dummy has spread any part of his hand.

A request to have calls restated should be responded to only by an opponent. Dummy or a player required by law to pass may review the auction at an opponent's request. Any player, including dummy or a player required by law to pass, may and should promptly correct an error in restatement.

21. *Call based on misinformation*

A player has no recourse if he has made a call on the basis of his own misunderstanding.

A player may, without penalty, change any call he may have made as a result of misinformation given him by an opponent, provided his partner has not subsequently called. If he elects to correct his call, his left-hand opponent may then, in turn and without penalty, change any subsequent call he may have made.

22. *Procedure after the auction is closed*

After the auction is closed:

A. If no player has bid, the hands are abandoned and the turn to deal passes in rotation.

B. If any player has bid, the final bid becomes the contract and play begins.

Irregularities

23. *Card exposed or led during the auction*

Whenever, during the auction, a player faces a card on the table or holds a card so that it is possible for his partner to see its face, every such card must be left face up on the table until the auction closes; and:

A. If it is a single card below the rank of an honor and not prematurely led, there is no penalty, and when the auction closes the card may be picked up.

B. If it is a single card of honor rank, or any card prematurely led, or if more than one card is so exposed, (penalty) the offender's partner must pass when next it is his turn to call; and if the offender subsequently becomes a defender, declarer may treat every such card as a penalty card (Law 50).

24. *Immediate correction of a call*

A player may substitute his intended call for an inadvertent call, but only if he does so without pause. If legal, his last call stands without penalty; if illegal, it is subject to the applicable law.

25. *Change of call*

A call substituted for a call made previously at the same turn, when it is too late for correction as provided in Law 24, is canceled; and:

A. If the first call was illegal, the offender is subject to the applicable law.

B. If the first call was a legal one, the offender must either

i] allow his first call to stand and (penalty) his partner must pass when next it is his turn to call; or

ii] make any legal call and (penalty) his partner must pass whenever it is his turn to call.

The offender's partner may also be subject to a lead penalty as provided in Law 26.

26. *Unauthorized information given by change of call*

When a player names a denomination not selected as his final call at that turn (as in changing a call* or in making or correcting an illegal call), then if he becomes a defender:

A. If such denomination was a suit, (penalty) declarer may prohibit the offender's partner from leading that suit the first time the offender's partner has the lead, including the opening lead, and for as long as he retains the lead.

B. If such denomination was no-trump, and if the offender's partner is to make the opening lead, (penalty) declarer may require the offender's partner to make the opening lead in a specified suit.

When a player has substituted another call for a double or redouble, the penalties provided in Law 27 (C) apply.

27. *Insufficient bid*

An insufficient bid made in rotation must be corrected, if either opponent draws attention to it, by substituting either a sufficient bid or a

---

* Except as permitted under Law 24.

pass.* A double or redouble may not be substituted. If the call substituted is

A. the lowest sufficient bid in the same denomination, the auction proceeds as though the irregularity had not occurred.

B. any other sufficient bid, (penalty) the offender's partner must pass whenever it is his turn to call.

C. a pass, (penalty) the offender's partner must pass whenever it is his turn to call; and if the offender's partner is to make the opening lead, declarer may either

i] require the offender's partner to lead a specified suit, or

ii] prohibit the offender's partner from leading a specified suit; this prohibition continues for as long as the offender's partner retains the lead.

If the offender attempts to substitute a double or redouble, it is canceled; he must pass and the offense is subject to the penalty provided in subsection C above.

If a player makes an insufficient bid out of rotation, Law 31 applies.

Call Out of Rotation

28. *Calls considered to be in rotation*

A call is considered to be in rotation

A. when it is made without waiting for the right-hand opponent to pass, if that opponent is required by law to pass.

B. when it is made by the player whose turn it was to call, before a penalty has been imposed for a call out of rotation by an opponent; it waives any penalty for the call out of rotation and the auction proceeds as though that opponent had not called at that turn.

29. *Procedure after a call out of rotation*

A call out of rotation is canceled if either opponent draws attention to it. The auction reverts to the player whose turn it was to call. The offender may make any legal call in proper turn but may be subject to penalty under Law 30, 31 or 32.

30. *Pass out of rotation*

When a player has passed out of rotation

A. before any player has bid, or when it was the turn of the opponent

---

* The offender is entitled to select his final call at that turn after the applicable penalties have been stated, and any call he has previously attempted to substitute is canceled, but Law 26 may apply.

on his right to call, (penalty) the offender must pass when next it is his turn to call.

B.   after any player has bid and when it was the turn of the offender's partner to call, (penalty) the offender must pass whenever it is his turn to call; the offender's partner may make a sufficient bid or may pass, but may not double or redouble at that turn; and if the offender's partner passes and subsequently is to make the opening lead, declarer may either

> *i*] require the offender's partner to lead a specified suit, or

> *ii*] prohibit the offender's partner from leading a specified suit; this prohibition continues for as long as the offender's partner retains the lead.

31.   *Bid out of rotation*
When a player has bid out of rotation

A.   before any player has called, (penalty) his partner must pass whenever it is his turn to call.

B.   after any player has called and when it was the turn of the offender's partner to call, (penalty) the offender's partner must pass whenever it is his turn to call; and if the offender's partner is to make the opening lead, declarer may either

> *i*] require the offender's partner to lead a specified suit, or

> *ii*] prohibit the offender's partner from leading a specified suit; this prohibition continues for as long as the offender's partner retains the lead.

C.   after any player has called and when it was the turn of the opponent on the offender's right* to call:

> *i*] If that opponent passes, the bid out of rotation, if sufficient, must be repeated and there is no penalty. If the bid out of rotation was insufficient it must be corrected as provided in Law 27.

> *ii*] If that opponent makes a legal bid, double, or redouble,† the offender may in turn make any legal call and (penalty) the offender's partner must pass when next it is his turn to call, and Law 26 may apply.

---

* A call made after any player has called and when it is the turn of the opponent on the offender's left to call is treated as a change of call and Law 25 applies.

† An illegal call by that opponent may be penalized in the usual way, after which this subsection C (*ii*) applies.

32.   *Double or redouble out of rotation*

When a player has doubled or redoubled out of rotation, and Law 36 or 37 does not apply:

A.   If it was the offender's partner's turn to call, (penalty) the offender's partner must pass whenever it is his turn to call; the offender may not thereafter, in turn, double or redouble the same bid he doubled or redoubled out of turn; and if the offender's partner is to make the opening lead, declarer may either

> *i*] require the offender's partner to lead a specified suit, or
>
> *ii*] prohibit the offender's partner from leading a specified suit; this prohibition continues for as long as the offender's partner retains the lead.

B.   If it was the turn of the opponent on the offender's right to call:

> *i*] If the opponent on the offender's right passes, the double or redouble out of rotation must be repeated and there is no penalty.
>
> *ii*] If the opponent on the offender's right bids, the offender may in turn make any legal call, and (penalty) the offender's partner must pass when it is his turn to call, and Law 26 may apply.

33.   *Simultaneous calls*

A call made simultaneously with one made by the player whose turn it was to call is deemed to be a subsequent call.

34.   *Call in rotation after an illegal call*

A call by a member of the nonoffending side after an illegal call by the opponent on his right, and before a penalty has been assessed, forfeits the right to penalize that offense. The illegal call is treated as though it were legal, except that an inadmissible double or redouble or a bid of more than seven is treated as a pass; and Law 35 or 37 may apply.

35.   *Retention of the right to call*

A player may not be deprived of any turn to call by one or more passes following a pass out of rotation, when there has been no subsequent bid. All such passes are canceled, the bidding reverts to the player who has missed his turn, and the auction continues as though there had been no irregularity.

Inadmissible Calls

36. *Inadmissible double or redouble*

Any double or redouble not permitted by Law 19 is canceled; and:

A.   If the offender has doubled or redoubled a bid that his side has already doubled or redoubled:

> *i*] The offender may substitute a legal bid, and (penalty) his partner must pass whenever it is his turn to call, and if the offender's partner is to make the opening lead, declarer may prohibit the lead of the suit illegally doubled or redoubled, for as long as the offender's partner retains the lead; or

> *ii*] The offender may substitute a pass, and (penalty) his partner must pass whenever it is his turn to call, either member of the nonoffending side may cancel all previous doubles or redoubles, and if the offender's partner is to make the opening lead, declarer may require the offender's partner to lead a specified suit, or prohibit the offender's partner from leading a specified suit; this prohibition continues for as long as the offender's partner retains the lead.

B.   If the offender has doubled a bid made by his side, redoubled an undoubled bid, or doubled or redoubled when there has been no bid, the offender in turn must make any legal call, and (penalty) his partner must pass when next it is his turn to call.

If the right of the nonoffending side to penalize is waived or forfeited, as provided in Law 15, the offender is deemed to have passed and the auction proceeds as though there had been no irregularity.

37. *Bid, double or redouble in violation of the obligation to pass*

A bid, double or redouble by a player who is required by law to pass is canceled, and (penalty) both members of the offending side must pass during the remainder of the auction, and if the offender's partner is to make the opening lead, declarer may either

A.   require the offender's partner to lead a specified suit, or

B.   prohibit the offender's partner from leading a specified suit; this prohibition continues for as long as the offender's partner retains the lead.

If the right of the nonoffending side to penalize is waived or forfeited, as provided in Law 15, the offender's bid, double or redouble, if otherwise legal, stands at that turn; but if the offender was required to pass for the remainder of the auction he must still pass at subsequent turns.

38. *Bid of more than seven*

A bid of more than seven by any player is canceled, and (penalty) both members of the offending side must pass during the remainder of the auction, and if the offender's partner is to make the opening lead, declarer may either

A. require the offender's partner to lead a specified suit, or

B. prohibit the offender's partner from leading a specified suit; this prohibition continues for as long as the offender's partner retains the lead.

If the right of the nonoffending side to penalize is waived or forfeited, as provided in Law 15, the offender must substitute a pass; any call that may have been made subsequently is canceled; and the auction proceeds as though there had been no irregularity. No play or score at a contract of more than seven is ever permissible.

39. *Call after the auction is closed*

A call after the auction is closed is canceled, and:

A. If it is a pass by a defender or any call by declarer or dummy, there is no penalty.

B. If it is a bid, double or redouble by a defender, (penalty) declarer may either

> *i*] require the offender's partner, when first it is his turn to lead, to lead a specified suit; or
>
> *ii*] prohibit the offender's partner, when first it is his turn to lead, from leading a specified suit; this prohibition continues for as long as the offender's partner retains the lead.

Part 6   The Play

Correct Procedure

40. *Commencement of play*

After the auction closes, the defender on declarer's left makes the opening lead. After the opening lead, dummy spreads his hand in front of him on the table, face up and grouped in suits with the trumps on his right. Declarer plays both his hand and that of dummy.

41. Information as to contract

After it is too late to have previous calls restated, as provided in Law 20, declarer or either defender is entitled to be informed what the contract is and whether, but not by whom, it was doubled or redoubled.

42. Dummy's rights and limitations

Dummy is entitled to give or obtain information as to fact or law; and provided he has not forfeited his rights (see Law 43) he may also:

A.   question players regarding revokes as provided in Law 61;

B.   draw attention to an irregularity, or try to prevent one.*

Except as provided in this law, dummy may not, on his own initiative, participate in the play, or make any comment on the bidding or play of the current deal, or draw attention to the score, and if he does so, Law 16 may apply. If dummy consults with declarer as to the imposition of a penalty, the right to penalize is forfeited as provided in Law 15.

43. Forfeiture of dummy's rights

Dummy forfeits the rights provided in A and B of Law 42 if he exchanges hands with declarer, leaves his seat to watch declarer play, or, on his own initiative, looks at the face of a card in either defender's hand; and if, thereafter,

A.   He is the first to draw attention to a defender's irregularity, declarer may not enforce any penalty for the offense.

B.   He warns declarer not to lead from the wrong hand, (penalty) either defender may choose the hand from which declarer shall lead.

C.   He is the first to ask declarer if a play from declarer's hand constitutes a revoke or failure to comply with a penalty, declarer must substitute a correct card if his play was illegal, and the penalty provisions of Law 64 apply.

44. Sequence and procedure of play

The player who leads to a trick may play any card in his hand.†

After the lead, each other player in turn plays a card and the four cards so played constitute a trick.

In playing to a trick, each player must if possible follow suit. This obligation takes precedence over all other requirements of these Laws. If unable to follow suit, a player may play any card.†

---

* He may, for example, warn declarer against leading from the wrong hand.

† Unless he is subject to restriction after an irregularity committed by his side.

A trick containing a trump is won by the player who has contributed to it the highest trump. A trick that does not contain a trump is won by the player who has contributed to it the highest card of the suit led. The player who has won the trick leads to the next trick.

45. *Card played*

Each player except dummy plays a card by detaching it from his hand and facing it near the middle of the table. Declarer plays a card from dummy's hand by moving the card toward the center of the table. If instructed by declarer to do so, dummy may play from his hand a card named or designated by declarer. In addition, a card must be played:

A.   If it is a defender's card held so that it is possible for his partner to see its face.

B.   If it is a card from declarer's hand that declarer holds face up in front of him and that is touching or near the table.

C.   If it is a card in dummy touched by declarer except for the purpose of arranging dummy's cards or of reaching a card above or below the card or cards touched.

D.   If the player who holds the card names or otherwise designates it as the card he proposes to play. A player may, without penalty, change an inadvertent designation if he does so without pause; but if an opponent has, in turn, played a card that was legal before the change of designation, that opponent may without penalty withdraw any card so played and substitute another.

E.   If it is a penalty card, subject to Law 50.

F.   If it is a card in dummy's hand that dummy has illegally suggested as a play, unless either defender forbids the play of such card, or an equal of it, or a card of the same suit, as provided in Law 16.

A card played may not be withdrawn except as provided in Law 47.

46. *Partial designation of a card to be played from dummy's hand*

When declarer instructs dummy to play a card from dummy's hand, as permitted by Law 45, but names only a suit or only the rank of a card, or the equivalent, without fully specifying the card to be played, declarer must complete his partial designation. Dummy must not play a card before declarer has completed his partial designation, and if dummy prematurely plays a card, Law 16 applies on that trick only, unless a defender has subsequently played.

47. *Retraction of a card played*

A card once played may be withdrawn only:

A.   to comply with a penalty, or to correct an illegal play;

B.   after a change of designation as permitted by Law 45 D;

C.   after an opponent's change of play, to substitute a card for one played.

Penalty Card

48. *Exposure of declarer's cards*

Declarer is not subject to penalty for exposing a card, and no card of declarer's or dummy's ever becomes a penalty card. Declarer is not required to play any card dropped accidentally.

When declarer faces his cards after an opening lead out of turn, Law 54 applies.* When declarer faces his cards at any other time, he is deemed to have made a claim or concession of tricks and Law 71 applies.

49. *Exposure of a defender's cards*

Whenever a defender faces a card on the table, holds a card so that it is possible for his partner to see its face, or names a card as being in his hand, before he is entitled to do so in the normal course of play or application of the law, (penalty) each such card becomes a penalty card (Law 50).

50. *Disposition of a penalty card*

A penalty card must be left face up on the table until it is played or is permitted to be picked up. When a penalty card is permitted to be picked up, it ceases to be a penalty card.

A penalty card must be played at the first legal opportunity, whether in leading, following suit, discarding, or trumping. If a defender has two or more penalty cards that can legally be played, declarer may designate which is to be played. The obligation to follow suit, or to comply with a lead or play penalty, takes precedence over the obligation to play a penalty card, but the penalty card must still be left face up on the table and played at the next legal opportunity.

When a defender has or first obtains the lead while his partner has a penalty card, declarer may require him to lead the suit of the penalty card or prohibit him from leading that suit for as long as he retains the lead.

---

* Declarer should, as a matter of propriety, refrain from spreading his hand.

If declarer exercises this option, the penalty card may be picked up. If declarer does not exercise this option, the defender may lead any card; but the penalty card remains a penalty card. The defender may not lead until declarer has indicated his choice.

If a defender has two or more penalty cards in one suit, and declarer requires the defender's partner to lead that suit, the defender may pick up every penalty card in that suit and may make any legal play to the trick.

If a defender has penalty cards in more than one suit, declarer may prohibit the defender's partner from leading every such suit; but the defender may then pick up every penalty card in every suit prohibited by declarer and may make any legal play to the trick.

51. *Penalty card illegally picked up*

When a defender attempts illegally to restore a penalty card to his unfaced hand, such card must be replaced face up on the table on demand of declarer; but if in the meantime that defender has played another card and declarer has thereafter played from either his hand or dummy, the card illegally picked up ceases to be a penalty card and need not be replaced on the table.

52. *Failure to lead or play a penalty card*

When a defender fails to lead or play a penalty card as required by Law 50, he may not, on his own initiative, withdraw any other card he may have played.

If a defender leads or plays another card when he could legally have led or played a penalty card,

A.   declarer may accept the defender's lead or play, and declarer must accept such lead or play if he has thereafter played from his or dummy's hand, but the unplayed penalty card remains a penalty card; or

B.   declarer may require the defender to substitute the penalty card for the card illegally led or played. Every card illegally led or played by the defender in the course of committing the irregularity becomes a penalty card.

Lead Out of Turn

53. *Lead out of turn accepted*

Any lead out of turn may be treated as a correct lead. It becomes a correct lead if declarer or either defender, as the case may be, accepts it or plays a card before attention is drawn to the irregularity. A card so played by declarer from either hand may not be withdrawn unless its play constituted a revoke. Law 57 applies if such card is played by the defender at the right of the player from whose hand the lead out of turn was made.

54.   *Opening lead out of turn*
When a defender makes the opening lead out of turn:

A.   If declarer accepts the lead as provided in Law 53, dummy's hand is spread in accordance with Law 40 and the second card to the trick is played from declarer's hand; but if declarer first plays to the trick from dummy's hand, dummy's card may not be withdrawn except to correct a revoke.

B.   If declarer may have seen any of dummy's cards (except cards that dummy may have exposed during the auction and that were subject to Law 23) he must accept the lead.

C.   If declarer begins to spread his hand as though he were dummy,* and in so doing exposes one or more cards, and if subsection B above does not apply, the lead must be accepted, declarer must spread his entire hand, and dummy becomes declarer.

When declarer requires the defender to retract his opening lead out of turn, Law 56 applies.

55.   *Declarer's lead out of turn*
When declarer leads out of turn from his or dummy's hand and either defender requires him to retract such lead:

A.   If it was a defender's turn to lead, declarer restores the card led in error to his or dummy's hand without penalty.

B.   If declarer has led from the wrong hand when it was his turn to lead from his or dummy's hand, he withdraws the card led in error; he must lead from the correct hand, and, (penalty) if able to do so, a card of the same suit. Failure to observe this obligation in playing from his own hand may subject him to penalty under Law 65.

Either defender's drawing attention to declarer's lead out of turn is equivalent to requiring its retraction. Dummy's drawing attention to declarer's lead from the wrong hand does not affect the rights of the opponents.

56.   *Defender's lead out of turn*
When declarer requires a defender to retract his lead out of turn:

---

* Declarer should, as a matter of propriety, refrain from spreading his hand.

A.   Declarer may treat the card illegally led as a penalty card and apply the provisions of Law 50; or

B.   Declarer may allow the card illegally led to be picked up; and if the offense occurred

> *i*] on the opening lead, or on a subsequent lead when it was the other defender's turn to lead, (penalty) declarer may require the offender's partner to lead the suit of the card led out of turn, or prohibit him from leading that suit for as long as he retains the lead.
>
> *ii*] when it was declarer's or dummy's turn to lead, declarer leads from the correct hand and (penalty) when first it is the turn of the offender's partner to lead, declarer may require him to lead the suit of the card led out of turn, or prohibit him from leading that suit for as long as he retains the lead.

Irregular Leads and Plays

57.   *Premature lead or play by a defender*

When a defender leads to the next trick before his partner has played to the current trick, or plays out of turn before his partner has played, (penalty) declarer may require the offender's partner to play:

A.   his highest card of the suit led; or

B.   his lowest card of the suit led; or

C.   a card of another suit, specified by declarer.

Declarer must select one of these options, and if the offender's partner cannot comply with the penalty selected he may play any card, as provided in Law 59.

When, as a result of the application of the penalty, the offender's partner wins the current trick, he leads to the next trick; and any card led or played out of turn by the other defender becomes a penalty card (Law 50).

A defender is not subject to penalty for playing before his partner if declarer has played from both hands; but a singleton or one of two or more equal cards in dummy is not considered automatically played unless dummy has played the card or has illegally suggested that it be played (see Law 45).

58.   *Simultaneous leads or plays*

A lead or play made simultaneously with another player's legal lead or play is deemed to be subsequent to it.

If a defender leads or plays two or more cards simultaneously, and if only one such card is visible, he must play that card; if more than one card is exposed, he must designate the card he proposes to play and each other card exposed becomes a penalty card (Law 50).

If declarer leads or plays two or more cards simultaneously from either hand, he must designate the card he proposes to play and must restore any other card to the correct hand. A defender who has played to the only visible card played by declarer may, without penalty, withdraw the card played and substitute another.

If the error remains undiscovered until both sides have played to the next trick, Law 68 applies.

59. *Inability to lead or play as required*

A player may play any correct card if he is unable to lead or play as required to comply with a penalty, either because he has no card of the required suit, or because he has only cards of a suit he is prohibited from leading, or because of his obligation to follow suit. The penalty is deemed to have been paid, except that the obligation to play a penalty card at the first legal opportunity continues.

60. *Play after an illegal play*

A play by a member of the nonoffending side after the opponent on his right has led or played out of turn or prematurely, and before a penalty has been assessed, forfeits the right to penalize that offense. The illegal play is treated as though it were legal, unless it constitutes a revoke. If the offending side had a previous obligation to play a penalty card or to comply with a lead or play penalty, the obligation remains at future turns (see Laws 52 and 65).

When a defender plays after declarer has been required to retract his lead out of turn from either hand, but before declarer has led from the correct hand, the defender's card becomes a penalty card (Law 50).

A play by a member of the offending side before a penalty has been assessed does not affect the rights of the opponents and may itself be subject to penalty.

The Revoke

61. *Failure to follow suit — Inquiries concerning a revoke*

Failure to follow suit in accordance with Law 44 constitutes a revoke. Any player, including dummy,* may ask a player who has failed

---

* Subject to Law 43. A claim of revoke does not warrant inspection of quitted tricks except as permitted in Law 67.

to follow suit whether he has a card of the suit led, and may demand that an opponent correct his revoke.

62. *Correction of a revoke*

A player must correct his revoke if he becomes aware of the occurrence of the revoke before it becomes established. To correct a revoke, the offender withdraws the card he played in revoking and follows suit with any card. A card so withdrawn becomes a penalty card (Law 50) if it was played from a defender's unfaced hand. The card may be replaced without penalty if it was played from declarer's or dummy's hand* or if it was a defender's faced card. Each member of the nonoffending side may, without penalty, withdraw any card he may have played after the revoke but before attention was drawn to it. The partner of the offender may not withdraw his card unless it too constituted a revoke.†

A revoke on the twelfth trick never becomes established, but it must be corrected if discovered before the cards have been mixed together, and declarer or either defender, as the case may be, may then require the offender's partner to play to the twelfth trick either of two cards he could legally have played to that trick.

63. *Establishment of a revoke*

A revoke in any of the first eleven tricks becomes established when the offender or his partner leads or plays to the following trick,‡ or names or otherwise designates a card to be so played, or makes a claim or concession of tricks orally or by facing his hand. The revoke may then no longer be corrected, and the trick on which the revoke occurred stands as played.

64. *Procedure after establishment of a revoke*

When a revoke has become established, (penalty) after play ceases, two tricks are transferred to the nonoffending side, if the side that has revoked has won two or more tricks after the revoke.§ Only one trick is transferred if the side that has revoked has won only one trick after the

---

* Subject to Law 43. A claim of revoke does not warrant inspection of quitted tricks except as permitted in Law 67.

† In such case the card withdrawn becomes a penalty card if it was played from a defender's unfaced hand.

‡ Any such play, legal or illegal, establishes the revoke.

§ Failure to lead or play a card or suit specified by an opponent in accordance with an agreed penalty is not a revoke but may be subject to the same penalties (see Law 65).

revoke. The trick on which the revoke occurred is counted as having been won after the revoke.* There is no penalty for an established revoke:

A.   If the side that revoked did not win either the trick on which the revoke occurred or any subsequent trick.

B.   If the revoke was a subsequent revoke in the same suit by the same player.

C.   If the revoke was made in failing to play any card faced on the table or belonging to a hand faced on the table including a card from dummy's hand.

D.   If attention is first drawn to it after all players have abandoned their hands and permitted the cards to be mixed together.

65. *Failure to comply with a lead or play penalty*

When a player is able to lead or play from an unfaced hand a card or suit required by law or specified by an opponent in accordance with an agreed penalty, but instead plays an incorrect card:

A.   The offender must correct his error if he becomes aware of it before he or his partner plays another card. Any card played in rotation by a member of the nonoffending side may be withdrawn, without penalty, if it was played after the error and before its correction. An incorrect card played from a defender's unfaced hand becomes a penalty card (Law 50).

B.   The offender may not withdraw any incorrect card he may have played if he or his partner has led or played to the following trick; and (penalty) the offense is subject to the penalty provisions of Law 64.

There is no penalty for failure to lead or play a faced card, including a penalty card† or a card from dummy's hand, but a member of the non-offending side (except dummy) may demand rectification at any time before a member of his side has thereafter played a card.

Tricks

66. *Collection and arrangement of tricks*

The cards constituting each completed trick are collected by a member of the side that won the trick and are then turned face down on the table. Each trick should be identifiable as such, and all tricks taken by a side should be arranged in sequence in front of declarer or of one de-

---

* For the scoring of tricks transferred see Law 80.

† A card played instead of the penalty card may be subject to penalty—see Law 52.

fender, as the case may be, in such manner that each side can determine the number of tricks it has won and the order in which they were taken.

67. *Inspection of tricks*

Declarer or either defender may, until a member of his side has led or played to the following trick, inspect a trick and inquire what card each player has played to it. Thereafter, until play ceases, quitted tricks may be inspected only to account for a missing or surplus card. After play ceases, the tricks and unplayed cards may be inspected to settle a claim of a revoke, of honors, or of the number of tricks won or lost. If, after a claim has been made, a player on one side mixes the cards in such way that the facts can no longer be ascertained, the issue must be decided in favor of the other side.

68. *Defective trick*

When a player has omitted to play to a trick, or has played too many cards to a trick, the error must be rectified if attention is drawn to the irregularity before a player on each side has played to the following trick. To rectify omission to play to a trick, the offender supplies a card he can legally play. To rectify the error of playing too many cards, the offender withdraws all but one card, leaving a card he can legally play. Each card so withdrawn becomes a penalty card (Law 50) if it was played from a defender's unfaced hand. After a card has been so withdrawn, each member of the nonoffending side may, without penalty, withdraw any card he played after the irregularity but before attention was drawn to it.

When attention is drawn to a defective trick after a player on each side has played to the following trick, the defective trick stands as played and:

A.   A player with too few cards plays the remainder of his hand with fewer cards than the other players; he does not play to the final trick (or tricks) ; and if he wins a trick with his last card, the lead passes in rotation.

B.   A player with too many cards forthwith faces and adds a card to the defective trick, and if possible one he could legally have played to it. A card so contributed does not change the ownership of the trick.

69. *Trick appropriated in error*

A trick appropriated by the wrong side must, upon demand, be restored to the side that has in fact won the trick by contributing the winning card to it. The scoring value of the trick must be credited to that side, subject to Law 81.

Claims and Concessions

70. *Declarer's claim or concession of tricks*

Declarer makes a claim whenever he announces that he will win or lose one or more of the remaining tricks, or suggests that play may be curtailed, or faces his hand. Declarer should not make a claim if there is any doubt as to the number of tricks to be won or lost.

71. *Procedure following declarer's claim*

When declarer has made a claim, play is temporarily suspended and declarer must place and leave his hand face up on the table and forthwith make a comprehensive statement as to his proposed plan of play, including the order in which he will play his remaining cards; and:

1] Either defender may, at any time thereafter, demand that declarer clarify or amplify his statement in any particular.

2] At any time after declarer's claim, either defender may face his hand for inspection by his partner and declarer may not impose a penalty for any irregularity committed by a defender whose hand is so faced.

3] Either defender may require that play continue as provided in Law 72.

Declarer's claim must be allowed if both defenders agree to it, or if either defender has allowed any of his remaining cards to be mixed with another player's cards.

72. *Continuation of play after declarer's claim*

Whenever either defender requires that play continue after declarer's claim, declarer must play on, leaving his hand face up on the table. Declarer may make no play inconsistent with any statement he may have made; and if he did not make an appropriate announcement at the time he made his claim, he may not exercise freedom of choice in making any play the success of which depends on finding either opponent with or without a particular unplayed card; and unless an opponent failed to follow to the suit of that card before the claim was made, declarer must play as directed by either defender. If declarer attempts to make a play prohibited under this law, either defender may accept the play or require declarer to withdraw the card so played and to substitute another that conforms to his obligations, provided neither defender has subsequently played. Any question not specifically dealt with should be resolved in favor of the defenders.*

73. *Defender's claim or concession of tricks*

When a defender makes a claim or concession of tricks he may do so by showing any or all of his cards to declarer only, but this does not necessarily exempt the defender from penalty under Law 16. If in the course of making a claim or concession a defender faces his hand, names a card as being in his hand, or makes it possible for his partner to see one or more of his remaining cards, his cards do not become penalty cards but declarer may treat the remaining cards of the other defender as penalty cards.

74. *Concession withdrawn*

A concession may be withdrawn:

A.   If any player concedes a trick his side has, in fact, won; or if declarer concedes defeat of a contract he has already fulfilled; or if a defender concedes fulfillment of a contract his side has already defeated. If the score has been entered, it may be corrected, subject to Law 81.

B.   If a trick that has been conceded cannot be lost by any sequence of play of the remaining cards, however improbable, and if attention is drawn to that fact before the cards have been mixed together.

C.   If a defender concedes one or more tricks and his partner immediately objects, but Law 16 may apply.

Part 7   The Score

75. *Points earned*

The result of each deal played is recorded in points, which fall into two classes:

1.   *Trick points.* Only declarer's side can earn trick points, and only by winning at least the number of odd tricks specified in the contract. Only the value of odd tricks named in the contract may be scored as trick points. (See Law 84.) Trick points mark the progression of the rubber toward its completion.

---

* *Example:* Declarer may be required to draw, or not to draw, an outstanding trump that he may have overlooked and that is a possible winner.

2.   *Premium points.* Either side or both sides may earn premium points. Declarer's side earns premium points by winning one or more over-tricks; by fulfilling a doubled or redoubled contract; by bidding and making a slam; by holding scorable honors in declarer's or dummy's hand; or by winning the final game of a rubber.* The defenders earn premium points by defeating the contract (undertrick penalty) or by holding scorable honors in either of their hands. (See Law 84.)

Each side's premium points are added to its trick points at the conclusion of the rubber.

76.   *Part score — game*

The basic units of trick scores are part score and game. A part score is recorded for declarer's side whenever declarer fulfills a contract for which the trick score is less than 100 points. Game is won by that side which is the first to have scored 100 or more trick points either in a single deal or by addition of two or more part scores made separately. No part score made in the course of one game is carried forward into the next game.

77.   *The rubber*

A rubber ends when a side has won two games. At the conclusion of the rubber, the winners of two games are credited in their premium score with 500 points if the other side has won one game, or with 700 points if the other side has not won a game. The trick and premium points scored by each side in the course of the rubber are then added. The side with the larger combined total wins the rubber, and the difference between the two totals represents the margin of victory computed in points.

78.   *Method of scoring*

The score of each deal must be recorded and preferably a member of each side should keep score.

Scores are entered in two adjacent columns separated by a vertical line. Each scorer enters points earned by his side in the left-hand column, and points earned by his opponents in the right-hand column.

Each side has a trick score and a premium score, separated by a horizontal line intersecting the vertical line. All trick points are entered, as they are earned, in descending order below the horizontal line; all premium points in ascending order above that line.

Whenever a game is won, another horizontal line is drawn under all trick scores recorded for either side, in order to mark completion of the

---

* For incomplete rubber see Law 83.

game. Subsequent trick scores are entered below the line so drawn. Any line prematurely drawn must be erased, and a line incorrectly omitted must be drawn upon discovery of the error.

79. *Responsibility for the score*

When play ceases, all four players are equally responsible for ascertaining that the number of tricks won by each side is correctly determined and that all scores are promptly and correctly entered.

80. *Transferred tricks*

A transferred trick is reckoned for all scoring purposes as though it had been won in play by the side to which it has been awarded.

81. *Correction of the score*

Any scoring error conceded by both sides may be corrected at any time before the score of the rubber is agreed upon; except that an error made by each scorer in recording a trick score, or failing to enter one, may not be corrected after the last card of the second succeeding correct deal has been dealt, unless the majority of the players consent. In case of disagreement among two or more scores kept, the recollection of the majority of the players as to the facts governs.

82. *Deals played with an incorrect pack*

Scores recorded for deals played with an incorrect pack are not subject to change by reason of the discovery of the imperfection after the cards have been mixed together.

83. *Incomplete rubber*

When, for any reason, a rubber is not finished, the score is computed as follows:

If only one game has been completed, the winners of that game are credited with 300 points; if only one side has a part score or scores in a game not completed, that side is credited with 50 points; the trick and premium points of each side are then added, and the side with the greater number of points wins the difference between the two totals.

	Odd Tricks Bid and Won in	Undoubled	Doubled
TRICK POINTS FOR CONTRACTORS	Clubs or Diamonds, each	20	40
	Hearts or Spades, each	30	60
	No Trump { first	40	80
	{ each subsequent	30	60

Redoubling doubles the doubled points for Odd Tricks.
Vulnerability does not affect points for Odd Tricks.
100 Trick Points constitute a game.

		Not Vulnerable	Vulnerable
PREMIUM POINTS FOR CONTRACTORS	*Overtricks*		
	Undoubled, each	Trick Value	Trick Value
	Doubled, each	100	200
	Making Doubled or } *Redoubled Contract* }	50	50
DEFENDERS	*Undertricks*		
	Undoubled, each	50	100
	Doubled { first	100	200
	{ each subsequent	200	300

Redoubling doubles the doubled points for Overtricks and Undertricks, but does not affect the points for making Doubled Contracts.

PREMIUM POINTS FOR CONTRACTORS|HOLDERS	*Honors in* { 4 Trump Honors	100
	One Hand { 5 Trump Honors or 4 Aces at No-Trump	150
	Slams Bid { Small, not vulnerable 500, vulnerable	750
	and Won { Grand, " " 1000, "	1500
	Rubber { Two game	700
	Points { Three game	500

Unfinished Rubber—Winners of one game score 300 points. If but one side has a part score in an unfinished game, it scores 50 points.
Doubling and Redoubling do not affect Honor, Slam, or Rubber points.
Vulnerability does not affect points for Honors.

Proprieties

I. *General principles*

Communication between partners during the auction and play periods should be effected only by means of the calls and plays themselves, not the manner in which they are made. Calls should be made in a uniform tone without special emphasis or inflection, and without undue haste or hesitation. Plays should be made without emphasis, gesture or mannerism, and so far as possible at a uniform rate.

Intentional infringement of a law is a serious breach of ethics, even if there is a prescribed penalty which one is prepared to pay. The offense may be the more serious when no penalty is prescribed.*

A player should carefully avoid taking any advantage which might accrue from an impropriety committed by his side. While one should not allow partner's hesitation, remark or mannerism to influence one's call, lead or play, it is not improper to draw inferences from an opponent's gratuitous hesitation, remark or mannerism, but such inferences are drawn at one's own risk.

There is no obligation to draw attention to an inadvertent infringement of law by one's own side; however, a player should not attempt to conceal such an infringement, as by committing a second revoke, concealing a card involved in a revoke, or mixing the cards prematurely.

It is proper to warn partner against infringing a law of the game, for example, against revoking, or against calling, leading or playing out of turn.

II. *Violations of ethical conduct*

The following acts should be carefully avoided and are considered breaches of ethics when committed intentionally. (a) A remark, question, gesture or mannerism which might convey information to partner or might mislead an opponent. (b) A call made with special emphasis, inflection, haste or undue hesitation. (c) A play made with emphasis, undue haste, or unreasonable delay, when the act might convey information to partner or might mislead an opponent. (d) Any indication of approval or disapproval of partner's call, or of satisfaction with an opponent's call. (e) Indication of expectation or intention of winning or losing a trick before the trick has been completed. (f) Mixing the cards before the result of the deal has been agreed upon. (g) A comment or act during

---

* See the Scope of the Laws.

the auction or play period, calling attention to an incident thereof, the state of the score, or the number of tricks already taken or still required.

III. *Observance of proper etiquette*

A player should maintain at all times a courteous attitude toward his partner and opponents. He should carefully avoid any remark or action which might cause annoyance or embarrassment to another player or interfere with the enjoyment of the game.

Every player should follow uniformly correct procedure in calling and playing, since any departure from correct standards may interfere with the orderly progress of the game.

A player should refrain from: (a) The use of different designations for the same call. (b) Frequent review of the auction or play due to his own inattention. (c) Volunteering information that should be given only in response to a question. (d) Looking intently at any other player during the auction or play periods, or at another player's hand as for the purpose of observing the place from which he draws a card. (e) Making gratuitous comments during the play period as to the auction or the adequacy of the contract. (f) Exchanging hands with his partner, or letting his partner see his hand, whether or not a penalty may be incurred. (g) Detaching a card from his hand before it is his turn to lead or play. (h) Disorderly arrangement of completed tricks, which may make it difficult to determine the sequence of plays. (i) Making a claim or concession of tricks if there is any doubt as to the outcome of the deal.

IV. *Use of conventions*

It is improper to use, in calling or playing, any convention the meaning of which may not be understood by the opponents. Conventional calls or plays should be explained to the opponents before any player has looked at his cards. Advance notice may be given of the intention to use certain conventions of which full explanation may be deferred until the occasion arises. The explanation may be given only by the player whose partner made the conventional call or play. At any time this player must reply to an inquiry by an opponent as to the significance of a call or play that may be conventional, and should supply any information that may have been withheld.

Any sponsoring organization, club or tournament committee, or group of persons playing Contract Bridge, may restrict the use of conventions in games under its jurisdiction.

v. *Spectators*

A spectator, or a member of a table who is not playing, should refrain from gratuitous remarks or mannerisms of any kind. He should not call attention to any irregularity or mistake, or speak on any question of fact or law except by request of a member of each side.